STUDY GUIDE

Seeing Angels

STUDY GUIDE

Seeing Angels

HOW TO RECOGNIZE AND INTERACT WITH YOUR HEAVENLY MESSENGERS

JOSHUA MILLS

WHITAKER
HOUSE

Seeing Angels Study Guide:
How to Recognize and Interact with Your Heavenly Messengers

International Glory Ministries
P.O. Box 4037
Palm Springs, CA 92263
JoshuaMills.com
info@joshuamills.com

ISBN: 978-1-64123-420-7
eBook ISBN: 978-1-64123-419-1
Printed in the United States of America
© 2019 by Joshua Mills

Whitaker House
1030 Hunt Valley Circle
New Kensington, PA 15068
www.whitakerhouse.com

1 2 3 4 5 6 7 8 9 10 11 〖Ⱳ〗 26 25 24 23 22 21 20 19

Contents

Introduction 7

How to Use this Study Guide 9

Part I: Understanding Your Angels

Lesson 1: Angels in Your Life 13

Lesson 2: Angels of Protection, Deliverance, and Comfort 19

Lesson 3: Angels of Healing 25

Lesson 4: Angels of Abundant Provision 31

Lesson 5: Angels of Divine Love 35

Lesson 6: Angels on Extraordinary Assignment 39

Lesson 7: Angels of Breakthrough and Revival 43

Lesson 8: Angels Over Churches, Cities, and Nations 49

Part II: Recognizing Your Angels

Lesson 9: Learning to Discern Your Angels 57

Lesson 10: Meeting Your Angels 63

Lesson 11: Your Angels Have a Name 67

Lesson 12: Angel Communications and Our Response 71

Part III: Working with Your Angels

Lesson 13: Commanding Your Angels 77

Lesson 14: Understanding Signs and Heavenly Messages 81

Lesson 15: Angel Movements and Atmospheric Shifts 87

Lesson 16: Spiritual Safety and Boundaries 91

Answer Key 97

Recommended Resources 109

Study to show yourself approved to God, a workman that needs not to be ashamed,
rightly dividing the word of truth.
—2 Timothy 2:15

Introduction

Suddenly, an angel of the Lord appeared among them,
and the radiance of the Lord's glory surrounded them.
—Luke 2:9 NLT

I believe that the Spirit has led you to this *Study Guide* to teach you the things of the Lord. The supernatural training and equipping you'll receive from these pages will come alive in you, as you begin not only to read and receive the revelation, but also to activate it within your own life.

This *Study Guide* will work as a companion tool alongside my book, *Seeing Angels*, so you will want to make sure you have both resources in your hands before you begin. The sixteen chapters from the book correlate with the sixteen lessons contained here in the *Study Guide*, but each lesson also contains additional learning material. Please take your time reading through the book and completing the assignments with each chapter. As you do, prepare yourself to learn, to be challenged, and to embrace new spiritual realities, as you engage with the revelation on these pages.

Although the topic and title of this *Study Guide* is *Seeing Angels*, my desire is that you would ultimately see Jesus Christ surrounding your life with His loving care and concern. God has given us access to his angels because He loves us dearly. My prayer is that you would know God's love, experience His love, and embrace His love through developing a healthy and authentic relationship with Jesus Christ. He is the Commander of the hosts of angels, and you will not be able to properly connect with them or with Him until you allow Jesus to be the Lord of your life. If you've never invited Him into your heart, to be your personal Lord and Savior, why not pray this prayer now?

> Jesus, come into my heart. I invite You to be my personal Lord and Savior. I give You my sin in exchange for the life that only You can give. Thank You for cleansing me with Your blood and giving me a brand-new start. I receive Your gift of salvation. Amen!

If you've just prayed that prayer by faith, you can be sure that Jesus now lives in your heart, and He will begin to help you in your spiritual journey. Make time to cultivate your personal relationship with Jesus Christ on a daily basis through developing your prayer life and a reflective time of Bible study (a good place to begin would be the book of John). God wants you to discover all that He has made available for you through Christ—including your angels!

Angels enhance our usefulness for God's service, and I am thankful for the angels God has allowed me to work with. The result has been that millions of people around the world have been able to hear the gospel message preached and have seen the evidence of that message demonstrated through signs, wonders, and miracles. In the process, my life has been blessed in countless ways.

It is my great joy and honor to welcome you now to join me in *Seeing Angels*. They are already surrounding your life, so together let's learn how to recognize and interact with your heavenly messengers!

—*Joshua Mills*
Palm Springs, California

How to Use this Study Guide

This *Seeing Angels Study Guide* can be used for either individual or group study.

TO FACILITATE A STUDY GROUP:

- Prepare your meeting space with peaceful, instrumental worship music, so that the atmosphere is set before the group begins to gather. We would recommend using Joshua Mills' SpiritSpa instrumental piano CDs (also available as digital music downloads online).

- Always begin the meeting with a simple prayer, asking God to direct the conversation and bring divine understanding from the words that are read. As part of your prayer, you could speak this scriptural blessing over the group from Ephesians 1:17–20 (NIV):

  I keep asking that the God of our Lord Jesus Christ, the glorious Father, may give you the Spirit of wisdom and revelation, so that you may know him better. I pray that the eyes of your heart may be enlightened in order that you may know the hope to which he has called you, the riches of his glorious inheritance in his holy people, and his incomparably great power for us who believe. That power is the same as the mighty strength he exerted when he raised Christ from the dead and seated him at his right hand in the heavenly realms.

- During the first meeting, ask each person to state their name and share their personal testimony in two minutes or less. Ask how everyone heard about the study group or why they are interested in learning about *Seeing Angels*. This will help the members of your group get acquainted with one another and feel at ease to participate.

- At all other meetings, ask questions to begin the conversation, such as:
  o "How did you like this week's chapter?"
  o "Is there something from the book that you would especially like to discuss?"
  o "Did anyone have a profound spiritual encounter (i.e. a dream, miracle, revelation, or angelic experience, etc.) through engaging with the concepts shared in the book?" (P.S. We would love to hear about them too!)

- For the group study, you can encourage participants to read the recommended pages in advance, or you can take turns reading aloud (depending upon your particular time restrictions and/or personal preferences).

- Try to keep the conversation centered on the book content, but realize that all the points in the *Study Guide* might not be covered during the meeting. Don't feel pressured by the *Study Guide*, but rather, see it as a facilitator for *Seeing Angels.*

- It is important to allow the Spirit to direct your conversations, so focus on the areas that He is leading you to focus on through the group discussion and the lesson content.

- Choose a corporate activity so everyone can directly engage with the revelation that has been shared within the specified lesson.

- When closing the meeting, you can do one or more of the following:
    o Use the last point in the study guide.
    o Lead or ask others to lead in a short closing prayer.
    o Sing a corporate worship song in theme with the discussion.
    o Thank everyone for coming.

- Sometimes group facilitators choose to offer simple refreshments at the end of a meeting as a way to encourage fellowship and develop deeper community. You may want to ask participants to take turns bringing in refreshments.

- Something you may want to consider is scheduling a special "Glory Celebration" after your last meeting, to commemorate your time together and make room to activate all the things you've learned. You could include a time of praise and worship, testimonies, and praying for one another, along with more food and fellowship.

FOR PERSONAL STUDY

- Find a place that is comfortable for you and prepare your personal space with peaceful instrumental worship music. This will set the atmosphere for you to easily read, learn, and receive from the Spirit. We would recommend using Joshua Mills' SpiritSpa instrumental piano CDs (They are available for digital download online).

- Always begin your time of study with a simple prayer, asking God to direct your thoughts and bring clarity of understanding from the words that are read.

- You can go through this curriculum at your own pace, but it is best to set a desired goal in order to keep yourself moving at a good pace. You will find momentum building as you read through each lesson, as each lesson builds upon the one before. There are a total of sixteen lessons in this *Study Guide.*

- Remember to activate each lesson through direct engagement with the revelation shared within that specific lesson.

- Most importantly,

Keep your eyes on Jesus…

Be anointed by His Spirit…

And begin Seeing Angels!

PART I

UNDERSTANDING YOUR ANGELS

"Believers, look up—take courage.
The angels are nearer than you think."
—Billy Graham

LESSON 1

Angels In Your Life

Before you begin this lesson, read chapter 1 in *Seeing Angels*.

For He shall give His angels charge over you, to keep you in all your ways.
—Psalm 91:11

1. Every believer has angels _____ to them, to perform certain _____ _____ to which they are called.

2. List some types of angels that are mentioned within the Scriptures:

   _____

   _____

   _____

   _____

3. The most important thing to remember is that there are _____ _____ assigned to *you*. Every place where an angel is mentioned in the Bible represents an area of your own life where an angel is available to work for you!

Definitions

4. The Hebrew word translated as *angel* in the Bible is *mal'ak* (Strong's H4397), which means "_____ _____ _____," "_____," or "____ _____ _____ __ _____."

5. The Greek word *aggelos* carries a similar meaning, denoting a "_____" or "_____ _____."

6. Have you ever experienced the presence of what you thought was an angel? If so, briefly describe that experience below. How did it feel, and what did it look like?

_____

_____

_____

_____

_____

7. When the Scriptures speak of angels, they are often mentioned in _____ _____. They have been called:

   + The _____ of heaven (See Revelation 19:14.)
   + _____ of fire (See Psalm 68:17; Zechariah 6:1–5.)
   + Heavenly _____ (See Psalm 103:21; 148:2; Luke 2:13.)
   + _____ ones (See Psalm 89:5, 7.)
   + An innumerable _____ (See Hebrews 12:22.)
   + _____ of God (See Job 1:6; 2:1.)
   + _____ (See Job 38:7; Revelation 12:4.)
   + _____ (See Daniel 4:13, 17.)

8. An old saying once stated that "Angels are to God what sunbeams are to the sun." This is correct in the sense that angels come from God, they are an extension of Him, and they release His heavenly radiance in the earth. What does this mean to you?

_____

_____

_____

Who is "The Angel of the Lord"?

9. One of the things that has puzzled biblical scholars and theologians for centuries is the use of the term *"the angel of the Lord"* throughout the Scriptures. On a few occasions in the Old Testament, this could have been Jesus Himself, appearing in Spirit form. This has been called a *theophany*, a manifestation or appearance of the pre-incarnate Christ. This would explain the angel's authority to _____ _____ (see Exodus 23:21), _____ _____ _____ (see Genesis 18:25), and _____ _____ from both Moses and Joshua (see Exodus 3:2–5; Joshua 5:14–15), for these are all things that only God can do.

10. We should, however, be careful to understand that this does not mean that Jesus is merely an angel. He is _____ than the angels (see Hebrews 1:4), He is the _____ and _____ _____ ____ _____ (see Hebrews 1:1–5), the angels _____ _____ (see Hebrews 1:6–7), and whereas angels are _____ heavenly beings (see Psalm 148:1–6), we know that Jesus has _____ for all of _____ (see John 1:1–14).

We also see the angel of the Lord appearing in New Testament times:

But while he thought on these things, behold, the angel of the Lord appeared unto him in a dream, saying, Joseph, you son of David, fear not to take to you Mary your wife: for that which is conceived in her is of the Holy Ghost. And she shall bring forth a son, and you shall call His name Jesus: for He shall save His people from their sins. (Matthew 1:20–21)

11. This angel's identity is not completely revealed in that passage, but Luke wrote about the angel _____ visiting Zacharias and Mary. (See Luke 1:11–20, 26–37.)

12. The angels we will be speaking about in this study are _____ _____, and God is not ____ _____.

The Wings of Angels

13. Some angels have wings, while others do not. Some have _____ wings, some have _____ wings (see Ezekiel 1:6), and some have _____ wings. Those extra wings cover their _____, _____, and _____ (see Isaiah 6:2).

14. The wings of some cherubim are awesome in appearance because they have _____ within those wings.

There are many Scriptures that symbolically speak about angels, comparing them to the birds of the air. The Scripture below speaks directly about the deliverance of God's people through angelic intervention:

You have seen what I did to the Egyptians. You know how I carried you on eagles' wings and brought you to myself. (Exodus 19:4 NLT)

Did you know that angels can supernaturally carry messages from one person to another? Consider this Scripture, for example:

Curse not the king, no not in your thought; and curse not the rich in your bedchamber: for a bird of the air shall carry the voice, and that which has wings shall tell the matter. (Ecclesiastes 10:20)

Angels can also fulfill specific spiritual duties and functions:

But she was given two wings like those of a great eagle so she could fly to the place prepared for her in the wilderness. There she would be cared for and protected from the dragon for a time, times, and half a time. (Revelation 12:14 NLT)

Holy Angels Reflect God's Glory

Angels carry the life essence of God and reflect His glory. They do not bring glory to themselves, but, rather, direct all glory to Jesus. For example, consider the mighty angelic creatures that Ezekiel saw:

As for the likeness of their faces, they four had the face of a man, and the face of a lion, on the right side: and they four had the face of an ox on the left side; they four also had the face of an eagle. (Ezekiel 1:10)

15. The Bible tells us clearly that they had four faces. Describe the revelation of each face in the chart on the next page:

The face of a MAN		John 1:14
The face of a LION		Numbers 24:9; Revelation 5:5
The face of an OX		Matthew 20:28; Mark 10:43
The face of an EAGLE		Deuteronomy 32:11; Job 39:27–29

Are Angels Male or Female?

16. Angels are _____ _____ with personal _____ _____.

It is possible for an angel to manifest in either male or female form, and the way God allows them to present themselves often speaks of their spiritual assignment on the earth.

17. The male gender is associated with _____, _____, and _____.

18. The female gender is associated with _____, _____, and _____.

CLASSES OF ANGELS
by Richard Sigmund

Angels in heaven also have different ranks and duties. For example, the Bible talks about the *"captain of the host of the Lord"* (Joshua 5:14 KJV) and *"Michael, one of the chief princes"* (Daniel 10:13). I saw at least seventy classes of angels in heaven. They follow their orders to the letter.

I first became aware of just how many classes of angels there were when I was walking on the golden pathway and smelled the fragrance that renewed my strength. I noticed more and more angels of every description and, I believe, of every rank. They were busy with the people, and they were beautiful and were everywhere. Some were in groups; others were by themselves. All were busy doing the business of heaven.

The classes of angels looked like they were family members. Some wore shirts with drawstrings. Some wore pants. Some had shoes. Their hair was never longer than their ears. None had a shaved head, but some had beards. They looked like they were about thirty in human years.

I saw some angels who looked twelve to fifteen feet tall and were as wide as four or five of the biggest linebackers on any NFL team. Some had swords, and some did not. But they were all huge. I was told that they were warfaring angels on their way to do battle. I stopped, bowed my head, and backed up a bit. But the angels with me and the voice behind me with a gentle touch (again, I believe this was Jesus) said, "You have nothing to fear. They are about the Father's business."[1]

1. Richard Sigmund, *My Time In Heaven* (New Kensington, PA: Whitaker House, 2004, 2010).

Different Types of Angels Mentioned in the Bible

19. In the history of Christianity, several theologians have set out to understand the celestial hierarchy by focusing on specific passages of Scripture[2] to develop an arrangement of three spheres, each one containing three orders of angels. Although the biblical canon is relatively silent on this subject, we know for sure that these heavenly beings differ in power with some having authority that others don't possess. Name the different types of angels in the chart below, and describe their function, ministry, or purpose:

THREE CELESTIAL SPHERES AND THE NINE ORDERS OF ANGELS Under the Lordship of Jesus Christ		
First Celestial Sphere (the Highest Heaven: the Third Heaven Dimension)		
		Psalm 104:4; Isaiah 6:1–7
		Genesis 3:24; Exodus 25:18–21
		Ezekiel 10:17; Daniel 7:9
Second Celestial Sphere (the Cosmic Heaven: the Second Heaven Dimension)		
		Ephesians 1:21; Colossians 1:16
		Ephesians 1:21
		Ephesians 3:10; 2 Thessalonians 1:7
Third Celestial Sphere (the Lower Heaven: the First Heaven Dimension))		
		Ephesians 1:21; 3:10
		Jude 1:9; 1 Thessalonians 4:16
		Psalm 34:7; Hebrews 1:14

Each class of angelic beings is different from the others, and they all serve their own individual purposes in the eternal plan of God.

---

2. Galatians 3:26–28; Matthew 22:24–33; Ephesians 1:21–23; Colossians 1:16.

20. Write out the declaration found on the last page of chapter 1:

_____

_____

_____

_____

_____

_____

_____

_____

_____

_____

_____

What part of this lesson stood out to you the most? How can you begin to apply this revelation to your daily life? Spend a few moments of reflection, writing down your thoughts:

_____

_____

_____

_____

_____

LESSON 2

Angels of Protection, Deliverance, and Comfort

Before you begin this lesson, read chapter 2 in *Seeing Angels*.

My God sent his angel, and he shut the mouths of the lions. They have not hurt me,
because I was found innocent in his sight.
—Daniel 6:22 (NIV)

1. God has given us angels of _____ and _____, just as He did
    for Daniel.

2. Why should a king get off of his _____ when he has plenty of _____ to do
    his bidding?

3. Kings _____ and _____, but then their _____ carry out
    those decrees and declarations. Likewise, God gives the _____, and the
    _____ hear those _____ and rush to carry them out.

4. Angels of protection are available in your life too. Where do you need these angels right now? How
    might they assist you?

    _____

    _____

5. You might think you have been waiting on _____ like that, but the truth is, _____ have
    been waiting on you! They move at the voice of their King.

6. What does Psalm 103:20 mean to you?

_____

_____

_____

_____

7. How is God's word heard on the earth today?

_____

_____

8. Name a few Bible verses that promise God's protection.

_____

_____

_____

_____

Unusual Angels in the Arctic

9. What can you do to activate angels in a desperate situation?

_____

_____

10. In his book, *Angels on Assignment*, Pastor Rolland Buck shared that the angel _____ spoke to him and said, "Read the Word; feed on it; let it become the Living Word to you, not just columns of truths and opinions of men."

11. What does that angel's revelation mean to you?

_____

_____

12. God has angels of protection for you too. When they come, they may come in some of the most extraordinary, unusual, and uncommon ways, but don't be guilty of _____ _____ _____ _____.

DELIVERED BY AN ANGEL
by William A. Ward

The first miracle that I remember was when I was four years old. I started to run across the street. An automobile came to a grinding stop as its wheels beat a protest against the pavement. The car almost hit me; the bumper stopped just short of my body. The driver got out of his car and grabbed me in his arms. He was shaking convulsively in every fiber of his being. He cried, "Where do you live?" I pointed to our house across the street. Still holding me in his arms, he went over and knocked on our door. My mother answered the door.

The man shouted, "You had better keep your boy off the street! I almost killed him. The only thing that saved your boy's life was a large, powerful angel who stood right in front of my car and held his hand up for me to stop. I did not see your son, but I had to jam on the brakes to keep from hitting the angel. As I came to a dead stop and ran around the car, there was your boy standing where the angel had been. You can thank that angel for saving your boy's life."

Tears flowing down her face, my mother held me on her lap and said, "William, just the other day a boy riding his motorcycle was hit by a car right where you were, and now you could have been killed, but God has protected you. You are chosen of God for His service. You belong to God. I dedicated you to Him before you were born. Please promise me that you will never allow a drop of beer, wine, or liquor to touch your lips. Always put God first in everything that you do." I answered, "I promise." Through the years I have kept that promise. I have never tasted anything stronger than Coca Cola. [3]

An Angel Saved My Daughter from Harm

13.   As you fill your home with _____ _____, you'll fill your life with _____ _____.

14.   There are angels available to protect your _____ _____ and _____ _____. There are angels available to protect your _____. There are angels available to protect your _____ and _____. There are angels available to protect your _____ and _____. There are angels available to protect your _____ and guard _____ _____ on your life.

ANGELS TO THE RESCUE

An interesting news story appeared in the *New York Daily News* several years ago:[4]

The officers who rescued a Utah toddler from death's doorstep in a submerged car on Sunday said their adrenaline-fueled heroics were triggered by a mysterious plea. "We could see a person in the front seat and then we heard a voice saying, 'Help me, we're in here.' It was clear as day," said Officer Tyler Beddoes of the Spanish Fork Police Department, one of four men who pulled an unconscious eighteen-month-old from a car—which had been submerged in near-freezing water for fourteen hours—as her mother lay dead in the driver's seat. Beddoes and his fellow first responders braved the chilly waters long enough to turn the red Dodge sedan, which was upside down, and pull little Lily Groesbeck out of her car seat, in which she had been suspended since her mother Jennifer Groesbeck apparently lost control of the car the previous evening.

"We could see her eyes fluttering, so there was some life, but as far as movements or consciousness, there was nothing that we could see," Beddoes told the *Daily News* on Monday. The four officers and three firefighters formed an assembly line and transported the child back to shore. The first responders started performing CPR, and Lily later regained consciousness in a Salt Lake City hospital. Her condition was upgraded to stable on Monday.

---

3. William A. Ward, *Miracles that I Have Seen* (Hagerstown, MD: McDougal Publishing, 1998).
4. *New York Daily News*, March 10, 2015, "'Mysterious Voice' led Utah cops to discover child who survived for 14 hours in submerged car after mom drowned," by Joel Landau

Jennifer Groesbeck, 25, was driving to her home in Springville, but when crossing a bridge in Spanish Fork, the single mom hit a cement barrier and drove off the roadway, police said. The vehicle crashed into the river around 10:30 p.m., according to a witness who told police he heard the accident. The car was not visible from the roadway, and was not discovered until 14 hours later, when a fisherman spotted it at 12:24 p.m. on Saturday and called police. That's when Beddoes and his partners arrived. The witness told them that he could see an arm through the window, and the four men plunged into the freezing rapids to see if they could find any survivors. Then, suddenly, they started hearing the distinct sound of a woman's voice, calling to them to help.

   "We replied back, 'Hang in there, we're trying what we can.'" The voice motivated them to push harder because they believed there might have been someone inside who was still alive. With their adrenaline pumping, they pulled the heavy, water-filled car onto its side and discovered the driver was dead. The officers had no explanation for the mysterious voice that appeared to come from inside the car. Beddoes said he wouldn't believe it really happened had not the other officers heard it as well. "I don't know what I thought I heard," he said. "I'm not a typically religious guy. It's hard to explain—it was definitely something. Where and why it came from, I'm not sure."

   The little girl was hanging upside down, but her head was not touching the water. The responders did not even see her, initially, but when they got the car turned over, they spotted her and raced to get her out. Groesbeck, the youngest of five children, was enrolled at Provo College and hoped to become a medical assistant, her sister Jill Sanderson told KSL-TV in Salt Lake City. "She was very compassionate and a very loving person and always willing to bend over backwards for her loved ones," she told the station. "Her baby was the love of her life. She was an amazing mother." The child was being treated at Primary Children's Hospital, where her condition was "stable and improving," a spokeswoman said Monday. "She is doing remarkably well considering the circumstance. The doctors have been hopeful so far," Sanderson told reporters. "We would like to express our appreciation to the Spanish Fork rescue team for saving the baby's life."

What was that mysterious voice the officers heard? It was the voice of an angel alerting the first responders to help! The article states that "they started hearing the distinct sound of a woman's voice, calling to them to help." The angel involved was directing them to the need. We'll never have full proof that this was an angel, but Officer Tyler Beddoes admitted that it could not be explained and stated: "where and why it came from, I'm not sure."

There are some things we simply cannot prove, but that's why God has given us faith. Faith gives us spiritual eyes to see into the unseen realm. Faith gives us spiritual ears to hear into the unheard realm. This is the way we are best able to receive the messages that God sends to us through angels. They come by faith.

Angels of Comfort

15. Have you ever felt the comfort of an angel in the midst of a difficult situation you were facing? Write down your thoughts on this.

   _____

   _____

   _____

16. God doesn't promise us that we won't have _____ in our lives. What we *are* promised is that _____ _____ will always be there with us. During _____ _____, these angels will help keep us balanced, so that we don't fall into pride. During _____ _____, they will help us navigate the path set before us with wisdom and grace, always reminding us of God's promises.

Angels Can Help Relieve Your Stress

17. During times of intense pressure, our _____ come to _____ _____ _____ and _____ ____ to be faithful in our commitments and responsibilities. When sudden _____ attempt to derail our lives, there are _____ who come to help bring recovery, ministering God's blessing.

18. What do the words of Isaiah 40:1 mean, when God said, *"Comfort, comfort my people"* (NLT)?

   _____

   _____

19. Stress and spiritual heaviness are the work of _____ _____ and they play a part in the onset of headaches, high blood pressure, heart problems, diabetes, skin conditions, asthma, arthritis, depression, and anxiety. When God's angels show up, they come to shift your atmosphere into one of _____ and heavenly _____.

What part of this lesson stood out to you the most? How can you begin to apply this revelation to your daily life? Spend a few moments of reflection, writing down your thoughts:

   _____

   _____

   _____

   _____

Angels of Healing

Before you begin this lesson, read chapter 3 in *Seeing Angels*.

*For an angel went down at a certain season into the pool, and troubled the water:
whosoever then first after the troubling of the water stepped in was made whole
of whatsoever disease he had.*
—John 5:4

1. Healing angels move between _____ and _____ to bring forth the manifestation of _____ in our lives. They come into our _____, _____, _____, and _____, bringing gifts of _____ and _____ of all kinds.

2. These angels heal anything: defective _____, damaged _____, deficient _____ _____, degenerated _____, _____ and _____ _____. Nothing is too difficult for God, and no health situation is too bleak for Him.

A Healing Angel in India

3. My late friend, Pastor Victor Gnanaraj, from Trichy, India, sent me a letter, telling of the great supernatural encounters he had been having:

   "...my prayer closet was filled with the presence of the Lord, and the Holy Spirit spoke to me expressly that _____ _____ are recruited for me: one of them being the _____ ____ _____, whose name is _____. He brings the _____ _____ from the cross of Calvary and deposits healing in sick people under my prayer requests to the Father. Ever since, miracles have happened, including fourth-stage cancer healed, kidney and gallbladder stones disappearing, etc."

4. Name the angels specifically mentioned within our Scriptures:
   + _____ ("warrior of God")
   + _____ ("hero of God")
   + _____ (the fallen angel meaning "adversary")
   + _____ ("the one who guards the bottomless pit")

5. Within some of the apocryphal texts, there appears another prominent angel named _____. This name means "_____ _____ ___ _____," as it is a combination of *rapha*, which means "healer," and *El*, meaning "God."

6. The root meaning of *Raphael* appears in the modern Hebrew word *rophe*, meaning "_____ ___ _____," again confirming the healing function traditionally attributed to this angel. Some ancient Jewish texts say that Raphael was the angel who taught Noah about _____ and _____ _____ _____ _____. It is believed by many (and I include myself in this number) that Raphael was the angel referred to in John 5:1–4 who _____ ____ the miracle waters in the _____ ____ _____. The exact name of the angel, however, is not as important as knowing his purpose.

HEALING ANGELS IN CHINA

In his book, *Heaven and the Angels*,[5] missionary H. A. Baker shared many testimonies about angels appearing on the mission field. This included some accounts of healing angels:

> A half-grown Ka Do tribal boy, visiting in a remote village, was asked by a sick woman, who had never heard of angels, to pray for her. As he prayed, the power of God came mightily upon both the boy and the sick woman. The woman saw a bright angel with wings. She was healed. In many instances, angels have been seen when the sick were divinely healed through prayer.

Concerning the healing of a woman who had been ill for some time, he wrote:

> She appeared to be in great darkness, when a light from above descended upon her, and two light-radiating hands and arms appeared. One of these hands was placed under her shoulders. With these kindly arms, she was gently raised into a sitting position. Her mother, who was near, was greatly surprised to see the sick woman suddenly arise and sit up. The woman was healed.

An Angel Delivers Gifts of Healing

7. In 1946, the famous evangelist William Branham had a life-changing encounter with a healing angel that imparted special supernatural gifts to him. These gifts would be used to carry God's healing power to people wherever Branham traveled. The angel told Branham, "God has sent you to take a _____ ____ _____ to the peoples of the world. If you will be sincere and can get the people to believe you, nothing shall stand before your prayer, not even cancer." Although

---

5. H. A. Baker, *Heaven and the Angels*, (New Kensington, PA: Whitaker House, 2014), 129.

William Branham's encounter was very unusual, and his prophetic gift and ability to discern specific illnesses has not been duplicated in recent years, people all over the world have reported _____ with God's _____ _____.

8. It seems to me that more angel encounters are happening _____ than ever before ____ _____ ____ _____. That makes sense because the pages of the final book of the Bible, the last-days book of _____, are filled with the greatest number of _____ _____.

9. Branham was a forerunner, but we have the privilege of continuing to run the race set before us. As our eyes are focused on Jesus, He will surround us with _____ _____ _____ everywhere we go. Jesus is the _____ _____, but His angels are the _____ _____.

ANGELIC WONDERS OF HEALING
by Brian Guerin

I have learned over the years that angels will actually tap you, nudge you, or brush you in exact body parts before you step into meetings to preach, signifying which precise physical needs for miraculous healing are going to be answered. I've seen this happen time and time again. I've seen this with deaf ears being opened, lungs being healed, barren wombs made alive, and so much more. The point here is that angelic beings are involved in God's purposes within the earth across the board. Many think that they are mere messengers alone. They certainly are that, but I would say "facilitators of heaven" would be a much more apt title. They get involved in just about every aspect of heavenly function, and we must realize this comes with eternal purposes. So next time you are about to go minister somewhere—or even if you're not in "ministry" and are about to step out into the marketplace—do not be surprised in the least if you are tapped, nudged, or brushed by angelic intuition, pointing you toward someone's dire need and an upcoming miracle.[6]

New Wine Angels

10. Several years ago, a group of _____ _____ showed up during one of my meetings at Winter Camp meeting in Ashland, Virginia. Each of these _____ _____ came into the room carrying what appeared to be an intravenous drip. God made it known to us, through a prophetic word, that instead of there being natural medicine inside their bags, these IVs were filled with supernatural "_____ _____."

11. These _____-_____ angels come to minister a _____ _____ of healing.

    Welcome God's healing angels into your life and learn how to cultivate an atmosphere for miracles to occur with ease.

Special Deliveries from Heaven

12. Because our angels are "_____ _____" sent to serve the heirs of salvation, they love to bring us special deliveries from heaven.

---

6. Brian Guerin, *God of Wonders* (Shippensburg, PA, Destiny Image: 2014).

13. Have you ever seen an angel bringing you a special delivery? Or have you sensed the presence of healing angels in your own life? Please explain:

_____

_____

_____

_____

Healing Angels Assist in Supernatural Surgery

14. What does Psalm 147:3 promise?

_____

_____

15. Your _____ is important to God, and He places a very high value on it. (See Proverbs 4:23.) Personally, I believe that He does some of His _____-_____ through the ministry service of angels.

16. Around the world, we often hear testimonies from people reporting that God has healed their hearts emotionally. Sometimes people have carried _____ _____, _____, _____, or _____ in their hearts for many years, and God wants to heal your heart from that too! I believe He has commissioned angels over your life to help you heal from _____ _____ and to encourage your heart to be open for all the love He desires to bring into your life today and tomorrow.

What part of this lesson stood out to you the most? How can you begin to apply this revelation to your daily life? Spend a few moments of reflection, writing down your thoughts:

_____

_____

_____

_____

_____

Activation #1: Decrees for Releasing Healing Angels

Step #1

Find a private, comfortable, and peaceful space where you can speak out the following Scriptures. Do it in a gentle but firm voice. Speaking these aloud will give you confidence that God wants to manifest healing for you.

You must serve only the LORD your God. If you do, I will bless you with food and water, and I will protect you from illness.
(Exodus 23:25 NLT)

Fear the LORD and turn away from evil. Then you will have healing for your body and strength for your bones.
(Proverbs 3:7–8 NLT)

The words of the wise bring healing. (Proverbs 12:18 NLT)

Dear friend, I hope all is well with you and that you are as healthy in body as you are strong in spirit. (3 John 1:2 NLT)

Step #2

Now, make these Scriptures very personal, by turning them into prophetic decrees over your life:

+ I will serve the Lord.
+ I receive divine protection from all illness.
+ I turn away from all evil.
+ I am healed in my body.
+ I receive strength in my bones.
+ I am wise with my words, and they bring healing.
+ I am well.
+ I am healthy in my body.
+ I am strong in my spirit.

As you do this, begin sensing the atmosphere changing around you. Your God-inspired words have invited the healing angels to gather around you. Take time to sense them right now. You may want to repeat Step #1 and Step #2 several times over, sensing the atmosphere being charged with angelic activity as you do. (This may feel like gentle peace or a warm blanket of love, or you may even begin seeing bright lights. Be open to all that God wants to bring you right now.

Step #3

Once you sense the healing angels around you, begin boldly commanding the healing angels to hearken unto the voice of God's Word. Say: "Ministering spirits, I send you to work right now in Jesus's name!" Feel free to customize this bold declaration, including stating the specific area of need that they are being dispatched to minister to.

Rest in the atmosphere of God's presence and let His Holy Spirit speak to you even as His healing angels minister for you.

Activation #2: Angelic Healing Waters

God's healing angels are willing and ready to minister to you right now. There is a beautiful, miraculous healing testimony found on the pages of John 5, but in that same chapter we also find additional insight regarding one of the ways that God can release healing into our lives through His angels. I want you to read it now:

Now in Jerusalem, near the Sheep Gate, there is a pool, which is called in Hebrew (Jewish Aramaic) Bethesda, having five porticoes (alcoves, colonnades). In these porticoes lay a great number of people who were sick, blind, lame, withered, [waiting for the stirring of the water; for an angel of the Lord went down into the pool at appointed seasons and stirred up the water; the first one to go in after the water was stirred was healed of his disease.] (John 5:2–4 AMP)

Now, I want you to experience these angelic healing waters for yourself. In order to complete this activation, you will need a partner. Choose which one of you will go first (you will be taking turns). Sit down in chairs facing each other, approximately five feet apart. One partner must relax in a comfortable position, while the other partner calmly reads the following paragraphs, being led by the Spirit to allow encounters and deep healing to occur.

Read:

I want you to close your eyes, and see the angels beginning to stir these healing waters once again for you right now. Allow yourself to relax. Let go of all worry, fear, and frustration. Just see these angels stirring the healing waters for you. See a healing pool that is being opened for you right now. See it being opened in front of you.

As you focus in the Spirit, you might see swirling lights or sense a flood of peace, love, and comfort. Open yourself to receive this true healing for spirit, soul, and body that comes from above. Angels of healing are being released to minister to your needs right now. They are stirring these spiritual waters for you. Notice the healing angels standing in these healing waters.

With your eyes closed, by faith, stand up and take a step into these miracle waters that are opening before you. Step all the way in, allowing yourself to be made holy and clean, as you are washed by the cleansing of God's word. (See Ephesians 5:26.) Feel the pure and cleansing water washing over you right now.

Now, reading partner, stand up and gently lay hands on the head or shoulder of your partner who is receiving. Then speak the following blessings over them:

- As you serve the Lord, you receive divine protection from all illness.
- You are healed in your body. Sickness and disease cannot prosper.
- You receive strength in your bones.
- You are well. You are healthy in your body. You are blessed.
- Receive your healing right now.
- Let the swirling healing waters of God surround your life right now.
- You are surrounded by God's love and His angels of healing.

Allow time for your partner to receive, then take turns doing it the other way around.

LESSON 4

Angels of Abundant Provision

Before you begin this lesson, read chapter 4 in *Seeing Angels*.

The blessing of the Lord, it makes rich, and He adds no sorrow with it.
—Proverbs 10:22

1. I have several angels of provision who travel with me and watch over the financial affairs of our family and our ministry. One of those angels is named _____.

2. God's angels are carriers who deliver God's blessings, but they are never the one from whom those blessings originate. That's why we must learn to always point our hearts and eyes toward _____.

Unusual Types of Provision

3. God has many angels of _____, angels of _____ _____, angels of _____ _____, and angels of _____, and each time they appear in the lives of God's people, they bring with them an array of unusual forms of provision. This would include the "angel food," the manna that God rained down on the Israelites as they traveled through the wilderness. (See Psalm 78:23–25.)

4. What types of unusual provision have you received in your own life? Please explain:

   _____

   _____

   _____

5. Do you think angels may have been involved these situations? Yes _____ No _____

6. The Bible makes it clear that our father Abraham was accustomed to having _____ ____ _____ lead him as he traveled in the land of Canaan (see Genesis 18:2; 22:11; 24:40). You and I can have the same blessing as Abraham. In other words, angels of blessing can come into our lives and lead us to the right place at the right time and to the right people. Praise God!

ANGELS OF ABUNDANCE

Jesus came to give you life, and He came to give it more abundantly! You were created to live the abundant life. The dictionary defines *abundance* as "overflowing fullness." I am comforted in knowing that God has angels assigned to our lives for the express purpose of giving us an overflowing fullness. These angels of abundance want to make sure that we are overflowing in spirit, soul, and body. They are not so much concerned with *how much* stuff you have, as they are with *what* stuff you have! Some people appear to own many material possessions and yet they are absolutely miserable, because the truth is: their material possessions own them. When your life is stifled and controlled by the things you own, that is not the abundant life. That is bondage to things. One of God's names is El Shaddai. He is the All-Sufficient One, and the abundance that God brings, fills you with His peace, joy, happiness, and supernatural satisfaction.

The Bible states that God will even give you the desires of your heart:

> *Take delight in the Lord, and he will give you the desires of your heart.* (Psalm 37:4 NIV)

When you get your heart right about abundance, God can take that and bless you with it. And He wants to bless you beyond anything you could possibly understand—even using angels in this way to bring exponential abundance into your life!

Angels Who Release Miracle Money

7. It is common for people to receive _____ _____ as they enjoy the presence of God.

8. Angels are constantly moving, activated by people's _____ _____ and by _____ God's Word over their finances.

9. God's angels are not hindered by harsh economic conditions or monetary recessions. They are released to _____ the financial atmosphere around you.

10. It doesn't matter who you are or where you live. Your current _____ _____ is not an obstacle for God. It's just another miracle waiting to happen.

Angels of Replenishment

11. God has angels that release miracle money for believers, and He also has angels that minister the supernatural replenishment of _____.

12. In 1 Kings 17, when the prophet Elijah asked a widow woman to use her limited supply of flour and oil to bake him a cake, the Scriptures tell us that although she used everything she had, *"no matter how much they used, there was _____ _____ _____ in the containers, just as the Lord had promised through Elijah"* (1 Kings 17:16 TLB). Although angels are not specifically mentioned in this passage (because that was not the focus of the story), I personally believe that _____ ____ _____ were involved in this miracle of divine supply.

13. Angels can _____ _____ _____ to minister supernatural overflow to those who are willing to receive it.

14. Everything we do in obedience to God becomes a seed for a future harvest. Something the Spirit has taught us is that we must make the connection between the _____ and the _____ worlds. God will ask us to do something _____ so that He can do something _____.

15. There is a _____ _____ between our generous giving on earth and the activation of our angels that bring supernatural provision from heaven.

What part of this lesson stood out to you the most? How can you begin to apply this revelation to your daily life? Spend a few moments of reflection, writing down your thoughts:

_____

_____

_____

_____

_____

LESSON 5

Angels of Divine Love

Before you begin this lesson, read chapter 5 in *Seeing Angels*.

And the LORD God said, It is not good that the man should be alone;
I will make him a help meet for him.
—Genesis 2:18

1. God desires for each and every person to find _____ _____ _____ _____ in their earthly life.

2. It was God Himself who said, *"It is not good for the man to be _____. I will make a _____who is just right for him"* (Genesis 2:18 NLT).

3. God never does anything without a purpose, and I truly believe that for each and every one of His promises, there are _____ assigned to help carry out that promise. For this reason, God has created a group of angels that I would classify as "_____ ____ _____ _____" because that is their God-given assignment—helping God's children find true love. Primarily, I am speaking here of each one finding a spouse to share life with.

4. Not only do these angels of divine love help people find a lasting _____ _____, but they also assist existing couples in _____ a loving and passionate marriage. In other words, they help _____ people together, and they help _____ people together.

Love Angels at Work in Hong Kong

5. Have you ever seen these types of angels before? If so, describe what happened:

_____

_____

6. After reading the testimony about these angels of divine love in Hong Kong, does it raise your expectation to encounter angels in other areas of your life as well? In what other personal areas of your life could you use the help of God's angels?

_____

_____

_____

_____

7. Should we be surprised that God's angels do their work? That's what they do. They work on your behalf, _____ _____ _____ _____ _____. They work to bring His purposes forth in your life, and since His purpose is for you to have a _____ _____, that's what they will work toward.

Angels of Divine Love for You

The Lord, the God of heaven, who brought me out of my father's household and my native land and who spoke to me and promised me on oath, saying, "To your offspring I will give this land"—he will send his angel before you so that you can get a wife for my son from there.   (Genesis 24:7 NIV)

8. These were the words of _____, spoken to his servant Eleazar, as he was giving him last-minute instructions before sending him out to find a proper bride for his son Isaac. God, he said, was also interested in this matter, so interested that ____ _____ _____ ____ _____ before Eleazar to prosper his way as he sought just the right bride for his master's son. The way Abraham spoke here makes me think that he was _____ to having angels work on his behalf. They must have guided him in the past. He was _____ _____ that this angel would do the work assigned to him, and he assured Eleazar of that fact.

9. Now, if these Old Testament figures could be aware of the _____ ____ _____ in their lives, how much more should we, all these years later, during this period of miraculous manifestation, experience angelic help from day to day. Believe for it.

A Heavenly Attraction

10. The way God creates divine relationships in your life is through attraction, not through strenuous effort on your part. He connects you with people who feel _____ ____ _____. It's all about the ease of God's glory. And that's what these angels will help you to do; they will lead you into that ease, which, in turn, will become attractive to others.

11. Nobody wants to be around a person who is _____, _____ _____, _____-_____, and _____ _____ _____ _____ _____. You are most attractive when you're living a life filled with joy and enjoying every moment of it. Remember, joy is more of a decision than it is a feeling. The angels of God make us aware of the joy of the Lord, which, in turn, becomes a supernatural strength—even when it comes to developing godly relationships.

12. List some types of people, blessings, or miracles that you would like to attract in your life:

_____

_____

_____

_____

_____

Now use the above list as a prayer tool to focus and ask God for His insight in attracting the right people and things to your life.

Love One Another

13. In our marriage, Janet and I have learned how important it is to _____ one another. It is essential to see the _____ that God has placed within your spouse. Instead of focusing on the negatives, look for the positive things that cause you to flourish together. Then, it is vital to communicate _____, _____ _____ to your spouse. Make this a daily habit. Tell your spouse how much you love him or her and how thankful you are for his or her presence in your life. When you do this, notice how the atmosphere begins to change in your home.

14. Let God lead you in _____ kind, affirming, positive _____ and scriptural _____ over your spouse and your marriage. Remember, angels are always waiting to hear God's Word being spoken from your lips, and that's what sets them in motion.

15. God's love is the best love, and when we share God's love with each other, it makes _____ _____!

16. Discuss your feelings with your spouse, but also make time to hear and really understand his or her feelings. Be willing to _____ if you've made a mistake, and be _____ ____ _____ each other. Living in this way ensures that you won't give any room to the devil. Instead, you will _____ _____ for your angels of divine love to work.

Learning to Flow Together

17. What is your difference? What makes you unique?

_____

_____

_____

18. As we find ourselves _____ ____ _____, we discover our full potential together ____ __ _____. God wants you to learn how to flow together _____ _____, so that you can flow together ____ __ _____. You can also learn to flow together with the _____ that have been assigned to your life, your marriage, and your ministry.

Three Things that Hinder Angels of Divine Love

19. I've often been asked, "What hinders angels of divine love from working within people's lives and marriages?" I've noticed three predominant areas as common threads when speaking with people who are suffering in this way. Name these three areas:

1. _____

2. _____

3. _____

What part of this lesson stood out to you the most? How can you begin to apply this revelation to your daily life? Spend a few moments of reflection, writing down your thoughts:

_____

_____

_____

_____

_____

LESSON 6

Angels on Extraordinary Assignment

Before you begin this lesson, read chapter 6 in *Seeing Angels*.

In the same way, there is joy in the presence of God's angels
when even one sinner repents.
—Luke 15:10 NLT

1. Angels often show up in ways we least expect. it has sometimes been in ways in which we didn't even know angels _____ act. We all have a lot to learn in this respect.

Angels Come to the Rescue

2. When we speak about all of the supernatural things that angels can do, I think it's essential to mention an important truth: the assignment of your angels is _____ ____ _____ _____ _____ _____ _____ from any given situation, but rather to make what seems _____ *naturally* _____ *supernaturally.* Angels are sent to us as ministering spirits, heavenly messengers, to partner with us in God's plans, purposes, and assignments for our life. But never expect an angel to do something that you can do.

3. If you _____ do a thing, then that's your _____. God doesn't send angels to us so that we can be _____. Actually, it's quite the contrary. He sends angels into our lives so that we will be much more _____ and _____ in fulfilling our life mission. The angels of God are standing ready to _____ in our lives whenever we need them.

4. David sang:

I sought the LORD, and he _____ me; he delivered me from all my fears. Those who look to him are radiant; their faces are _____ _____ _____ _____. This poor man called, and the LORD heard him; he saved him out of all his troubles. The angel of the LORD

_____ _____ *those who fear him, and he* _____ *them.*

(Psalm 34:4–7 NIV)

5. Notice what David said: *"he answered me."* God hears our _____. He not only heard David, but he also delivered David from all of his fears. And God's promise is that *"the angel of the LORD encamps around those who fear him, and he delivers them."* God's angels are not only ready to help us with the concerns of our daily lives; they are _____ _____ to aid and assist us in _____ _____ _____ _____ in all the earth.

6. God has _____ _____ of angels.

FEARLESS
by Charity Virkler Kayembe

A characteristic we immediately notice about angels is their incredibly confident nature. While completely humble, they are entirely bold and brave. They have not a hint of arrogance, but they are absolutely assured that whatever they are intending to do will be accomplished, because they have God backing them up. They don't have anything to prove to anybody; they just live to please Father.

Angels are also extraordinarily positive and give new meaning to the words eternal optimist! They have no fear. No pride. No stress. No doubt. It is such an awesome amalgamation, that extreme humility and extreme confidence. They have the revelation that we have won, that it is already done. (See Colossians 2:9–15.) Jesus secured our victory and the Most High really is Ruler over the realm of mankind. (See Daniel 4:17.)

That version of reality is all angels see. All they know is God's truth and His perspective. The war has already been won, so they never fight for victory. They always, only, naturally, exclusively fight from a position of victory.

All of that is what we're going for. In so many ways, how they live is what we aspire to. And where else would we see an example of this (by someone who is not God Himself [Jesus]—except for in angels? We don't know anyone who is perfect. Here is our chance to see in real time what it can actually look like. Feel like. Sound like.

When we see our angels in action, we get a vision for holiness and how awesome it is, and that makes it seem a little bit more within reach. When we walk with the wise, we become wise, and if even just a tiny bit of that glory rubs off on us, we are a lot better off than when we started.[7]

An Angel Bakes a Power Cake

7. Throughout the Scriptures, we see angels at work in the lives of God's people ____ _____ _____. One such angel appeared to Elijah and baked him a cake, giving him _____ _____ to eat. This power cake became strength for the journey ahead of him. The Scriptures show that this "angel food" enabled Elijah to travel, strengthened in

---

7. Charity Virkler Kayembe and Joe Brock, *Everyday Angels*, (Shippensburg, PA: Destiny Image, 2018), used by permission.

this miraculous way, for _____ days and _____ nights until he reached Mount Sinai. (See 1 Kings 19:5–8.)

The Finding Angels

8. I believe that all of God's angels work to bring us into the blessing that He has provided through the finished work of Christ, but there seem to be some angels who are _____ with the specific task of helping us to _____ _____ _____ that have gone missing. I believe that these are our guardian angels, the ones that watch over us on a continual basis. They also serve as "_____ _____" because they care about every important detail of our lives.

    When we ask God for His help, these angels get to work, assisting us to find whatever has been lost. This can include _____ _____ that hold sentimental value (i.e., Jewelry, photos, etc.), _____ _____ ____ _____, _____ _____ _____, _____, and even _____ _____.

9. It's fun to see your _____ returning your missing items to places where you are certain you never left them. One lady got back a missing _____ _____ that had been lost for ten years! Jesus said, *"Ask, and it shall be* _____ ___.*"*

10. When we are driving through an overcrowded parking lot, we ask God to send His angels to _____ ____ __ _____ _____ _____. And it works! Sometimes that perfect parking space is up front, close to the buildings, and we're thankful for it. At other times, that perfect parking space is at the back of the lot, and we realize that God is giving us an opportunity to exercise and remain healthy! We rejoice in both situations! God _____ _____ _____.

    What part of this lesson stood out to you the most? How can you begin to apply this revelation to your daily life? Spend a few moments of reflection, writing down your thoughts:

    _____

    _____

    _____

    _____

    _____

Angels of Breakthrough and Revival

Before you begin this lesson, read chapter 7 in *Seeing Angels*.

But the angel of the Lord by night opened the prison doors, and brought them forth.
—Acts 5:19

1. Breakthrough angels can come to minister to us in the realms of _____
_____, _____, and _____ _____. They intervene for
_____, _____, and _____ _____ _____
_____, and they often produce _____ _____ in dire
circumstances. Like all other angels, they can take on many different appearances, as the Spirit
allows. Expect it and rejoice in it.

Fireballs of Breakthrough in Victoria, BC

2. Every time we _____ and _____ _____ _____ ____ _____ _____, angels are
released in accordance with that Word. Let go of all _____, all _____,
and all _____, and begin to cooperate with heaven's purposes. If you need a breakthrough in
your life right now, begin speaking _____ _____ ____ _____.

3. Although Peter was securely locked up in prison, we can see in the Bible what happened when the
church began to pray and speak with faith:

   Suddenly an angel of the Lord _____ and a light shone in the cell. He struck Peter
   on the side and _____ _____ ____. "Quick, get up!" he said, and the chains fell off Peter's
   wrists.   (Acts 12:7 NIV)

4. *"Suddenly,"* a breakthrough angel appeared in Peter's prison cell. This means that Peter
wasn't necessarily expecting it at that particular moment in time. The appearance of the

angel was _____. It all happened in an instant. God delights in bringing us His "_____."

5. The angel who came to Peter had to wake him up. As Peter came out of sleep, there was a strange light in his cell, and he saw a stranger standing before him, saying, "_____, _____ ____!" Next, the chains were falling from his wrists. It all happened so *suddenly*.

6. When your angel of breakthrough gives you instructions from heaven, _____ _____ and _____ _____ _____. Move immediately in _____ to those instructions, and do whatever the angel is telling you to do.

7. God sends angels with divine _____. He sends angels to _____ preachers and ministries. He sends angels with _____ _____. (See Acts 8:26.) God's angels bring _____ messages, and their words will always line up perfectly with His _____ _____. They will bring a _____ of the things that God has already been revealing to you by His Spirit.

A Breakthrough Angel in Sonora, California

8. This angel had been sent on _____ _____ to prepare regions for revival.

9. What was the three-word message this angel said to tell the people? "_____, _____, _____!"

10. It doesn't matter how difficult a situation might seem in the natural, when a _____ _____ comes, and you partner with that angel, something *will* break through. Breakthrough angels have been released from _____. Are you willing to let them work in you?

ANGELS GUARD A REVIVAL
by Dr. Roy H. Hicks

In his book, *Guardian Angels*, Dr. Roy H. Hicks related one of the many stories he heard Aimee Semple McPherson share regarding the ministry of angels, from the time he spent sitting under her ministry over many years. In his own words, I wanted to share the story with you here:

"She first began her ministry as a young woman on the East Coast, using a gospel tent. As she related it, she arrived at a certain city, and the people who assisted her had unknowingly pitched the tent on some property that was used as a place for the local young men to play baseball. She was told this, but it was too late to change plans. They had to go ahead as planned, at least for the first night.

As the service began, she saw the angry young men coming from the bushes around the tent. They were carrying gasoline cans, and she knew they intended to burn the tent.

She relates, "I said to the Lord, 'What shall I do?'" The Lord told her to lift her hands and begin to worship Him. As she obeyed, her eyes were opened in the Spirit and she saw the tent completely surrounded by a host of angels with their wings extended and touching, wing tip to wing tip. As she opened her eyes, she saw the men, all with looks of astonishment on their faces. They dropped the cans and stood there with mouths agape. Later on, many of them began to attend the services, and many were saved.

When Angelus Temple, the beautiful church seating 5,300 people, which Mrs. McPherson built in Los Angeles, California, was erected, she had the painters stencil angels wing tip to wing tip, around the perimeter of the auditorium just under the huge dome to commemorate the event.[8]

Angels of Harvest

11. There are also _____ ____ _____, some who reap on their own and others who assist us in the harvest. John the Revelator wrote about them:

> Then another angel came out of the temple and called in a loud voice to him who was sitting on the cloud, "Take your _____ and _____, because the _____ ____ _____ has come, for the harvest of the earth is _____."
> (Revelation 14:15 NIV)

12. In these last days, we have a great responsibility at hand. We have been _____ by Jesus to go into all the earth, proclaiming the Good News of the gospel and reaping __ _____ ____ ____ _____. We can't do this on our own, nor does God expect us to. Are you willing to learn how to work with _____ _____ ___ _____? They are available for you.

Angels Work With Us

13. God wants His glory and miracles to surround us continually, so He has provided the assistance of _____ _____, but we must be willing to work with them. If the person an angel is assigned to becomes _____, that angel will go looking for someone more willing to _____ _____ the things of God.

An Atmosphere Shift in Singapore

14. Wherever I go, the glory is _____ _____ _____. Even in the most difficult regions and under the most troublesome situations, we have still experienced the visitation of the glory of God.

15. What seemingly insurmountable problem did I face when I arrived to minister at an Anglican church in Singapore?

_____

_____

16. Did this seemingly impossible situation hinder God? _____

17. Very often someone will comment to me: "I can feel the _____ whenever you minister, and it feels so _____ than anything else I've experienced in my life." That lets me know that God's angels are working with us. God has given us His angels to help us make it happen.

---

8. Dr. Roy H. Hicks, *Guardian Angels* (Tulsa, OK: Harrison House, 1991).

An Angel Named Swift

18. What is the name of the angel assigned to the prophetic ministry of my friend, Patricia King, and why is he named that?

_____

_____

19. The Bible describes how Philip had an angel appear to him, to help _____ _____ to his ministry:

> *And the angel of the Lord spoke to Philip, saying, Arise, and go toward the south to the way that goes down from Jerusalem to Gaza, which is desert.*   (Acts 8:26)

20. God is able to send the ministry of His breakthrough and revival angels to us in _____ _____ _____. Sometimes they come in the most _____ and _____ ways!

Supernatural Oil, Angel Voices, and Heavenly Music

21. What unusual manifestations happened in Big Bear Lake, California, at the Mountain Top Encounter?

_____

_____

_____

_____

_____

_____

_____

_____

_____

_____

_____

_____

_____

22. What were the two words God spoke to me about those meetings?

_____   _____

23. That day marked a new beginning of _____ all over the world, and people in many places entered into a new season of _____.

What part of this lesson stood out to you the most? How can you begin to apply this revelation to your daily life? Spend a few moments of reflection, writing down your thoughts:

_____

_____

_____

_____

Angels Over Churches, Cities, and Nations

Before you begin this lesson, read chapter 8 in *Seeing Angels*.

And I saw another angel fly in the midst of heaven, having the everlasting gospel to preach unto them that dwell on the earth, and to every nation, and kindred, and tongue, and people.
—Revelation 14:6

1. We've already seen in the Bible that angels have been assigned over our personal lives, but did you realize that there are also angels assigned over your _____, over your _____, and over your _____?

2. There are angels specifically assigned to help with the work of ministry. They partner with _____, _____, _____, and _____. There are also angels specifically assigned to individual churches. These angels oversee _____ _____, _____, and _____ _____, and they desire to _____ _____ _____ succeed in their calling. Sometimes these angels are assigned to bring a specific word or direction to the church they are called to.

3. In what chapters of Revelation are these angels mentioned in relation to specific churches? _____ ____ and _____ ____

4. Because the Greek word *angelos* means "messenger," some theologians have struggled with this supernatural idea, proposing instead that these "messengers" may just have been _____ or _____ over the church. Are these messengers human? Or could it be possible for heavenly messengers to watch over individual churches? We see John clearly answering this question by precisely stating:

The mystery of the seven stars which you saw in My right hand, and the seven golden candlesticks: The seven stars are _____ _____ ____ _____ _____ _____: and the seven candlesticks which you saw are the seven churches. (Revelation 1:20)

5. I believe that God used the apostle John, while he was exiled on the isle of Patmos, to write messages _____ ____ these seven angels. Then the angels would bring the messages and share them with the respective church _____. It is also significant to note that John emphasized how important it was for the church to *"hear what the Spirit says to the churches"* (Revelation 2:7 NIV). These messages clearly were not _____ the angels; the angels were simply _____ _____ _____ for God's message to be given to the churches.

6. Also notice that the *"stars"* were held in Jesus's right hand. In the Scriptures, the right hand represents _____, _____, _____, and _____. (See Exodus 15:6; Psalm 20:6; 98:1.) These are all attributes that God has given to our guardian angels. In the same way that we each have personal guardian angels, the Lord has made provision for each and every _____ to have a guardian angel.

7. It's interesting to note that the very last words of Jesus recorded in the Bible were about the ministry of an angel in the church. In Revelation 22:16, he said: *"I Jesus have sent _____ _____ to testify to you these things in the churches."* These angels are there to help the pastor and the church members to fulfill their purposes as a congregation of believers.

The City of Angels

8. Los Angeles is known as the "_____ ____ _____." The name *Los Angeles*, in Spanish, literally means "_____ _____." I don't think it's a coincidence that God chose this physical location to birth the modern move of His Spirit at the turn of the twentieth century. Anytime God wants to show up and manifest Himself, His angels always seem to be involved. Look at the evidence we can find for this in the Scriptures:

   + God created the earth in the _____ of angelic hosts singing His praises. (See Job 38:4–7.)

   + An angel manifested in the midst of the _____ _____, representing the victory of God's people. (See Daniel 3:13–29.)

   + An angel army set an _____ against the enemies of Israel, allowing Jehoshaphat and his men to win the war. (See 2 Chronicles 20:22.)

   + An angel told Zacharias that his wife, Elizabeth, would bear a son ____ _____ _____ _____. (See Luke 1:13.)

   + An angel appeared to Mary to announce that she would _____ the Christ child. (See Luke 1:30–31.)

   + Angels descend from heaven to announce _____ _____ to the shepherds in the fields of Judea. (See Luke 2:10–14.)

   + Women, followers of Jesus, saw a vision of angels who told them _____ _____ _____. (See Luke 24:23.)

   + Two angels dressed in white garments declared the _____ ____ _____. (See Acts 1:10–11.)

   + Angels of "wind" and "fire" _____ ____ _____ for the arrival of the Holy Spirit. (See Acts 2:2–4.)

9. The Bible reminds us:

For we wrestle not against flesh and blood, but against _____ , against _____ , against the _____ of the darkness of this world, against _____ _____ in high places. (Ephesians 6:12)

10. There are both _____ and _____ angels who preside over regions, and the Scriptures tell us that they fight against one another. (See Revelation 12:7–10.)

11. God's people need to understand more about angels and how to empower them over churches, cities, and nations through _____ , _____ , and _____ .

ANGELS BLOW THEIR TRUMPETS OVER THE CITY!

Frances Hunter, shared a testimony about seeing these church angels blowing their trumpets and the exciting results this produced:

"Look at all those angels standing on the roof of the church!" I exclaimed as we drove from the airport in Fargo, North Dakota, to the First Assembly of God Church where we were to start a Healing Explosion. "Look! Look! Look! There are angels standing on all four sides of that church! There are angels stationed all the way around the roof, and they're all blowing trumpets, calling people in from the North, the South, the East, and the West! Isn't that exciting!"

The church building has a flat roof, and, in the Spirit, I could see all four sides at one time. The pastor, who was driving, said, "That really sends goose pimples up and down my spine because just this morning in the prayer meeting, we asked God to bring them in from the North, South, East, and West for the Healing Explosion! This confirms what we prayed this morning!"

When the time came for the Healing Explosion to start, God's angels had blown those trumpets so clearly that people streamed in from all four directions. For the first time in the history of the city of Fargo, they had a traffic jam! Fargo is not a really big city, but so many thousands of people came to the Healing Explosion they had to park their cars in the surrounding cornfields! When angels get busy on their trumpets, watch out! Things happen!

God Creates Boundaries and Supervising Angels

God Most High gave land to every nation. He assigned a guardian angel to each of them, but the LORD himself takes care of Israel. (Deuteronomy 32:8–9 CEV)

12. God literally created boundary lines, and when He created separate nations in the earth, according to *The Living Bible*, "He gave each of them a _____ _____ ."

13. Nations were created around certain angelic _____ , angelic _____ , angelic _____ , and angelic _____ . In

other words, when an angel goes to war, the nation that angel represents also goes to war. The laborers in Christ's vineyard must understand the things that are happening in the spirit world. There is a spiritual influence that is creating the natural realities we can see in the flesh. What we are seeing is real enough, but it is _____ _____ a spiritual source. Paul wrote to the Ephesian believers:

> *Finally, my brethren, be strong in the Lord and in the power of His might.* (Ephesians 6:10)

14. This is a prophetic command to each of us. *"Be strong in the Lord and in the power of his might."* It continues in the next verses: *"Put on the whole _____ ____ _____, that you may be able to stand against the wiles of the devil"* (verse 11). Who is our enemy? It is the devil and his fallen angels, and we must be able to stand against his _____, his _____, and his _____. We must stand and take our place in the kingdom of God. Why? *"For we do not wrestle against flesh and blood"* (verse 12).

15. Oh, if we could just stay in _____ _____! That's the very best place to be. That's where you will learn to work with your angels. That's the place where you can learn to _____ in the loving arms of Jesus, knowing that He is the Prince of Peace. (I strongly encourage you to read my book, *Moving in Glory Realms*, as it lays the basic foundation for everything I am sharing here. These concepts can be clearer and more fully understood through the revelation set forth in that book.) God is looking for someone who will be willing to get into the glory and push things through by His Spirit. He is looking for true believers.

16. In Daniel's time, the Jewish people were held _____, _____ by the Persian Empire. Daniel, therefore, got on his knees and began talking to the Lord in prayer. He began pushing this thing through in the realm of the Spirit—pushing, pushing, and pushing some more. He pushed like this for three weeks.

17. Daniel later wrote:

> *Then I lifted up my eyes, and looked, and behold a certain man clothed in linen, whose loins were girded with fine gold of Uphaz: his body also was like the beryl, and his face as the appearance of lightning, and his eyes as lamps of fire, and his arms and his feet like in color to polished brass, and the voice of his words like the voice of a multitude. And __ _____ _____ saw the vision: for the men that were with me saw not the vision; but a great quaking fell upon them, so that they fled to hide themselves.* (Daniel 10:5–7)

It is interesting that Daniel said, *"I Daniel alone saw…."* Often, when angels make their appearance, regardless of how glorious or magnificent they may seem, you might be the only one to see them. But even if you're the only one seeing an angel, don't discount what the Lord is allowing you to see. The Bible says that there were other men in the room with Daniel, but they failed to see what Daniel saw. They did, however, feel the presence of the Lord. According to the Bible, something made the other men flee. They could feel the weight of God's _____.

18. When the angels of God begin to make their appearance, there is a realm of glory that comes with them. That glory realm comes ____ _____ _____. When you begin interacting with angels, that heavenly realm comes upon you. It can also come upon a _____, a _____, or an entire _____. It comes as an impartation that others will begin to sense, discern, and pick up on. You, among others, will be changed by it.

19. Daniel continued:

And, behold, a hand touched me, which set me upon my knees and upon the palms of my hands. And he said unto me, O Daniel, a man greatly beloved, understand the words that I speak to you, and stand upright: for to you am I now sent. And when he had spoken this word to me, I stood _____. (Daniel 10:10–11)

In verse 20, the angel said: *"Do you know why I have come? Soon I must return to fight against the spirit prince of the kingdom of Persia, and after that the spirit prince of the kingdom of Greece will come"* (NLT). This verse mentions three different angelic beings that represent three different nations: _____, _____ and _____. Just as each nation has _____ angels who have been assigned to it, each also has _____ angels who have been assigned to it.

The Angels of the Nations

20. God has created a group of angels who interact in the affairs of _____ _____. I call these "_____ _____ ____ _____ _____" because they watch, stand guard over, and respond to the prayers of God's people in a particular nation. They also help bring direction.

21. St. Patrick, the national apostle of Ireland, had a well-known nighttime encounter with an angel known as _____. In a dream, this angel delivered to him a letter entitled, "The Voice of the Irish," which deeply moved him and eventually gave him the confidence to boldly spread Christianity throughout Ireland.

ANGELS WATCH OVER ISRAEL
by Mahesh and Bonnie Chavda

What happens in the politics of your nation will affect, and will be affected by, you. Part of your spiritual calling is authority as an ambassador of heaven within the boundaries of your national citizenship. Pray that good men and women will rule in your nation so that holy angels will have access to and influence in your land. Pray that your national leaders will be servants of the Lord and friends of Israel. In fact, a sure way to bring blessing to a nation is for the saints to intervene in prayer, not only for the peace of Jerusalem, but also for their nations to be friends of Israel.

We know many firsthand reports of angelic intervention in the battle for Israel still today. Our friend Tsvi, who served in the Israel Defense Force, told us of an amazing victory made possible with the help of angels on assignment. He was one of only a hundred Israeli soldiers left to defend an outpost in the Sinai, guarding the southern entrance to Israel.

They watched as Egyptian tanks filled the plain below their post. The Israeli soldiers went on high alert, ready to defend their position 24/7 for the first few days of the Egyptian mobilization. The Israeli soldiers were outnumbered and had only a limited amount of ammunition left. With tension mounting, they waited.

Days passed and the Egyptians did not make a move to strike. Puzzled, the Israelis continued to watch, but began to allow soldiers to sleep in shifts. Finally, to their amazement and relief, the thousands of invaders suddenly turned and retreated. That tiny outpost was the only natural barrier between Israel and the invading army, but they turned back home without a fight. Our friend told us that it was just like in the Bible. God sent His invisible forces to stand before them and confuse the mind of the enemy. God-of-the-Angel-Armies is now turning His heart toward "home" to keep His promise to gather Israel into His bosom, as He told Abraham He would do thousands of years ago.[9]

22. God has a _____ _____ _____ _____ for every nation, as varied and diverse as they are in so many ways. God recognizes each of them, loves each of them, and has purposes for each of them.

23. God watches over His Word to perform it, and you can be used by God to _____ _____, _____ _____, and _____ _____, as you learn how to work with the angels of the nations.

What part of this lesson stood out to you the most? How can you begin to apply this revelation to your daily life? Spend a few moments of reflection, writing down your thoughts:

_____

_____

_____

_____

_____

9. Mahesh Chavda and Bonnie Chavda, *Storm Warrior* by (Grand Rapids, MI: Chosen Books. 2008).

PART II

RECOGNIZING YOUR ANGELS

"Make yourself familiar with the angels and behold them frequently in spirit,
for without being seen, they are present with you."
—St. Francis de Sales

LESSON 9

Learning to Discern Your Angels

Before you begin this lesson, read chapter 9 in *Seeing Angels*.

…some have entertained angels unawares.
—Hebrews 13:2

1. What did Georgia's angel do for her and her husband?

   _____

   _____

   _____

2. The great revivalist Jonathan Edwards once said, "The seeking of the kingdom of God is the chief business of the Christian life." It's God's desire for you to engage with the _____ _____. I can guarantee you that He doesn't want you to be left out in the cold concerning angels, and that is why He so freely offers us the gifts of the Spirit.

3. As you learn to spiritually discern angels, it is important to focus your complete dependence upon the Lord Jesus Christ. He is the _____ _____ who promises to lead us in the paths of righteousness in the glory realms. His rod, representing authority, and His staff, representing support, will bring us _____ and _____ as we begin to explore these realms. All wisdom, sight, and perception must flow from our personal relationship with _____. He has a gift that He wants to give to each and every one of us, and that is the gift of "*discerning of spirits*" (1 Corinthians 12:10).

4. In the same verse, the *Amplified Bible, Classic Edition* calls this gift: "*the ability to _____ and _____ _____ [the utterances of true] spirits [and false ones]*." By the Spirit, we can know what is _____ and what is _____, what has _____ motivation and what is motivated by the _____, what is from _____ and what is from the _____. This

gift includes, but is not limited to, sensing the spirit realm and its beings. When discerning in this way, you will not be operating in your own natural understanding. What comes to you will come through a supernatural awareness. Discerning spirits is accomplished through the power of the Holy Spirit, as He bears witness with our spirit when something is or is not of God.

5. Too many people are spiritually _____ in the church. Their eyes have been closed, and their spiritual vision has been _____. But the Scriptures are clear: God wants us to see openly and with accurate precision—in all circumstances and situations—in order to fully manifest our God-given potential. We need to know the truth, and the discerning of spirits gives us that ability.

6. As we have noted, whether you've been aware of it or not, angels _____ _____ _____ on a daily basis. Hopefully, this study has given you some insight into these angels already, but having the ability to discern spirits will make you fully aware of their presence and intent—and allow you to cooperate more perfectly with them.

7. Ruthann had long been frightened by the thought of seeing an angel. Describe what happened when she changed her mind and wanted this experience:

   _____

   _____

   _____

8. Too many people are blocked by _____—fear of others, or fear of the unknown—blocked by their natural limited _____, or blocked by their natural _____. Some people have been blocked by _____ _____ _____ of what they think an angel should look like or by what they've been told an angel should appear. The Bible clearly warns us to be careful because we may be entertaining angels unaware. (See Hebrews 13:2.) This shows us that angels can either look just like us or they can come in a form that we don't immediately recognize at all.

9. Sometimes angels are sitting, standing, or dancing among us, and ____ _____ _____ _____ for who they are. Because angels are spirit beings and can present themselves in very unusual ways, we need the Spirit's help to be able to _____ them properly.

THE SOUND OF ANGEL MUSIC
by Maria Woodworth-Etter

In her book, *Signs and Wonders*, Maria Woodworth-Etter shared about a time in Petoskey, Michigan, when the angels began to sing, and the heavenly orchestra started playing supernatural music:

The heavenly choir was glorious. It was as if heaven had come down, and the angelic choir had joined in with the redeemed of the Lord, having many invisible instruments. Musical instruments (spiritual) were heard way back to the rear of the tent. A thousand or more were present. A holy stillness and a spirit of awe settled over the audience; they knew that God was in their midst.

Two or three different times, I asked the people to answer me honestly, in the fear of God, if they heard different instruments of music from the platform. The sounds were not given on instruments, but by the Spirit. I knew they had heard it. I asked all who had heard the heavenly music or instruments to rise in the presence of God. Men and women rose up here and there, clear to the back of the tent.

Once, when the power of God was wonderfully present, I heard a sister's music; looking around, I saw a sister (an evangelist) with eyes uplifted to heaven, her face shining, playing the harp in the Spirit. She said the glory of the Lord covered her, and the Lord placed a golden harp in her hands. Her fingers began to play, bringing forth the heavenly sound. Several others were playing on different instruments, sending out heavenly music.[10]

10. In addition to this gift, we can also learn how to be aware of the presence of angels by looking for clues throughout _____ _____. Also, I believe that God wants to give you three spiritual disciplines that will help you to cooperate with this gift of discerning spirits that has now been given to you. This will enable you to discern your angels.

11. Name the spiritual disciplines we need to discern the presence of angels and describe each one in your own words.

_____

_____

_____

_____

_____

_____

12. The doorway to the supernatural is through your _____, not through your _____.

13. Discerning spirits gives us the ability to see past the _____ and into _____ realities. It allows us to become aware of spiritual truths that surround us. Paul wrote:

So we fix our eyes not on what is seen, but on what is _____, since what is seen is temporary, but what is unseen is _____. (2 Corinthians 4:18 NIV)

14. The _____ realm is the most real realm.

15. In regard to spiritual insight, the Bible says we see ____ _____ and we prophesy ____ _____. The *New Living Translation* renders that verse in this way:

Now our knowledge is _____ and _____, and even the gift of prophecy reveals only _____ of the whole picture! (1 Corinthians 13:9)

---

10. Maria Woodworth-Etter, *Signs and Wonders* (New Kensington, PA: Whitaker House, 1997), 354.

HOW TO DISCERN THE SPIRITS
by Mary K. Baxter

How are we to know if what presents itself as an angel is truly from God? The Bible tells us to try or test the spirits to see if they are authentic:

Dear friends, do not believe everyone who claims to speak by the Spirit. You must test them to see if the spirit they have comes from God. For there are many false prophets in the world. This is how we know if they have the Spirit of God: If a person claiming to be a prophet acknowledges that Jesus Christ came in a real body, that person has the Spirit of God. But if someone claims to be a prophet and does not acknowledge the truth about Jesus, that person is not from God. Such a person has the spirit of the Antichrist, which you heard is coming into the world and indeed is already here. (1 John 4:1–3 NLT)

If we continually read and meditate on the Word of God, we can distinguish between the devil's deceiving angels and God's holy angels. You can tell whether or not an angel is from God by what he says about the Lord Jesus and the salvation He provided for humanity when He came to earth as a man and shed His precious, cleansing blood on the cross. If a spiritual being communicates any message that denies the deity, humanity, or salvation of the Lord Jesus, we can unmask him as the enemy. We can expose him through the power of the Holy Spirit. If his message promotes an unscriptural message or practice, if it draws attention to himself rather than Jesus, then that spirit being is a demon attempting to deceive people.

Therefore, if any being, or any person, claiming to be an angel begins to tell you something that is different from God's Word, or that goes against God's Word, you can know that an evil spirit from hell is behind it. Remember that Satan twisted the Scriptures out of context when he tried to tempt Jesus in the wilderness (see Luke 4:1–13), and he is still trying to manipulate the Scriptures to deceive people today. Make it a priority to study and learn the whole Word of God so you can tell when the Scriptures are being misquoted.

While fallen angels are working as hard as they can to do evil under the direction of the devil, righteous angels are diligently serving God and doing good under His direction. God's holy angels continually glorify Him. They acknowledge Jesus Christ and His coming into the world to redeem us from the enemy's bondage. They focus on Jesus and His deliverance. By their activities and actions, they continually emphasize God' work and will."

Both a Gift and a Discipline

16. Spiritual sight is both a _____ to be received and a _____ to be developed. We can practice and grow in discerning spirits:

    But solid food is for the mature, who by constant use have _____ _____ to distinguish good from evil. (Hebrews 5:14 NIV)

17. Practice your spiritual _____. Practice your spiritual _____. Practice your spiritual _____. Then repeat the process on purpose.

18. I want to give you faith to understand that it is totally possible for you to come into a place of being aware of _____ _____ every single day of your life, every single minute of every single day, and every place you go—no matter the life circumstances.

What part of this lesson stood out to you the most? How can you begin to apply this revelation to your daily life? Spend a few moments of reflection, writing down your thoughts:

_____

_____

_____

_____

_____

_____

LESSON 10

Meeting Your Angels

Before you begin this lesson, read chapter 10 in *Seeing Angels*.

For the angel of the Lord is a guard; he surrounds and defends all who fear him.
—Psalm 34:7 NLT

1. When I was a child, seeing angels seemed _____ because I and other young church friends could see them in a very vivid way.

2. What hindered my ability to see angels?

   _____

   _____

Childlike Faith Restored

3. Speaking about faith, Jesus said: *"Truly I tell you, unless you change and become _____ _____ _____, you will never enter the kingdom of heaven"* (Matthew 18:3 NIV).

4. If we want to enter into these supernatural kingdom realities, we must return to a _____ _____ .

5. Many people feel as though their _____ _____ has been lost because of life experiences in their past, perhaps due to trauma, abuse, and any number of other reasons. I believe God both wants to and has the ability to restore your faith like that of a child.

6. I have created an acronym using the word CADET to best describe the individual elements of childlike faith. According to the dictionary, the archaic meaning for the word *cadet* is "a young _____ or _____ ."

7. Fill in the meaning beside each letter of the acronym CADET.

C	
A	
D	
E	
T	

8. Explain in your own words what it means to be confident in God and why that is important.

_____

_____

9. Explain in your own words what it means to be awe-inspired and why that is important.

_____

_____

10. Explain in your own words what it means to be discovering and why that is important.

_____

_____

11. Explain in your own words what it means to be expectant and why that is important.

_____

_____

12. Explain in your own words what it means to be tenacious and why that is important.

_____

_____

13. The Spirit will train us and open divine connections for us, as we allow Him to restore our _____ _____ and help us to become a CADET believer. Our childlike faith aligns us to receive the insight and obtain our spiritual promises as we move forward.

A Sanctified Imagination

14. These days, when I mention the word imagination, it is frowned upon by most Christian believers. They assume that I'm talking about having a thought that does not correspond to the reality of things in the "real world." But your imagination is simply _____ _____ _____ ____ _____ _____. It is the part of you that connects with the unseen world, but that world is very real indeed. Just because it is unseen to your natural eyes doesn't mean that it doesn't exist. There are many things that we cannot see with our eyes; this is why God has given us an imagination, the part of us that is able to see beyond mere earthly realities.

15. Consider this: everything that has ever been created was first _____. Your imagination is God's gift to you, and in the Scriptures, we are instructed to have the mind of Christ. (See Philippians 2:5.) Do you believe that Jesus could see much more than what was naturally presented before Him? I do. I personally believe that was why He was able to walk on water, walk through walls, work miracles, prophesy with accuracy, know the hearts of men, and ultimately journey to the cross of Calvary.

16. The Bible declares: "…*who for the* _____ *that was set before Him endured the cross, despising the shame…*" (Hebrews 12:2). The joy that was set before Jesus had to be a vision or picture that He could see in His imagination. It certainly wasn't a natural vision of the agony and terror that He would face.

17. Define the word *imagination*:

    _____

    _____

18. Many in the church have been afraid of this realm because of the words of 2 Corinthians 10:5, which speak of "*casting down* [_____] *imaginations.*" Let's look at that Scripture for a moment to see what it's really speaking about:

    Casting down imaginations, and every high thing that exalts itself against the knowledge of God, and bringing into captivity every thought to the obedience of Christ.

19. This is a powerful instruction, encouraging us to cast down "_____ _____ _____ *that exalts itself against the knowledge of God.*" Our imaginations must be _____ and brought into _____ to God and His ways. If the apostle Paul felt strongly enough to address this issue, it must have been because he understood the power of our imagination.

Three Biblical Ways Our Angels Appear

20. Name the most common ways that angels appear to us and give an example of each:

    _____

    _____

    _____

21. How have angels appeared to you?

    _____

    _____

When you begin seeing glimpses of your angels through visions or dreams, take note of their appearance, what they are holding in their hands, how they are dressed, specific colors, or anything else that may be important for understanding their mission.

Angels Among Us

22. Have you begun to use your Angels Among Us Tracking Sheet from chapter 10 of *Seeing Angels?* Yes __ No __. If so, what has been the result? If not, I encourage you to do that.

_____

_____

23. What did an angel do for us one day on the streets of Hollywood, California?

_____

_____

Meeting My Guardian Angels

24. How did my guardian angels first appear to me?

_____

What part of this lesson stood out to you the most? How can you begin to apply this revelation to your daily life? Spend a few moments of reflection, writing down your thoughts:

_____

_____

_____

_____

_____

Your Angels Have a Name

Before you begin this lesson, read chapter 11 in *Seeing Angels*.

Surely goodness and mercy shall follow me all the days of my life:
and I will dwell in the house of the Lᴏʀᴅ for ever.
—Psalm 23:6

1. Here David referred to his angels by name, calling them "_____" and "_____." Had you ever noticed that before? David wasn't just speaking about the attributes of God here; he was speaking about two guardian angels whom he knew had been assigned to his life.

Angels Reveal Their Name in a Dream

2. Who was Dana and why did it surprise me?

   _____

   _____

3. Dana is a Hebrew name that means "_____ ____ _____." This was extremely significant to us as a family because we were young and very new to the ministry, and yet God was doing profound (some would say "controversial") supernatural things in our lives. We had begun experiencing many unusual signs, wonders, and miracles, which seemed to bring us much persecution everywhere we went. We were often misunderstood and wrongly accused. What an encouragement to know that God had placed His angel, Dana, in the center of our lives!

4. It reminded us that God has the _____ _____, and it gave us the confidence to move forward in the ministry assignment set before us.

Angels Named Joy and Abundance

5. Offering someone your _____ is the very first step toward developing a _____ with them. This is the way we introduce ourselves to others, and we should expect our angels to do the same when they are introducing themselves to us.

6. What you'll discover about your angels is that when you meet them, they will never _____ _____ ____ _____. Their names carry a ministry assignment from God, and this, in itself, should direct your attention back to the Lord.

What's Your Angel's Name?

"I am Gabriel. I stand in the presence of God, and I have been sent to speak to you."   (Luke 1:19 NIV)

7. Scripturally, you can ask your angel about its name, and I think you should. When Manoah inquired of the angel who visited him about his name, he responded by telling Manoah it was _____. (See Judges 13:17–18.) Angels with descriptive names like _____, _____, _____ are obvious in their assignments to deliver what their name implies. But sometimes the name and meaning don't seem so obvious and will require a bit of research and inquiring of the Holy Spirit to understand.

8. What type of angel was Chrioni?

_____

9. What was the special assignment of Swift?

_____

10. What was the purpose of Caramat, Zimri, and Ryan?

_____

_____

_____

11. What is your angel's name?

_____

"Ask and You Shall Receive"

Ask, and it shall be given you; seek, and you shall find; knock, and it shall be opened to you.

(Matthew 7:7)

12. When is a good time to ask your angel his name?

_____

_____

13. The name Greg means _____ _____ _____!" What type of angel was Greg?

_____ _____ _____

What part of this lesson stood out to you the most? How can you begin to apply this revelation to your daily life? Spend a few moments of reflection, writing down your thoughts:

_____

_____

_____

_____

_____

LESSON 12

Angel Communications and Our Response

Before you begin this lesson, read chapter 12 in *Seeing Angels*.

The people therefore, that stood by, and heard it, said that it thundered: others said,
An angel spoke to Him. Jesus answered and said,
This voice came not because of Me, but for your sakes.
—John 12:29–30

1. Have you ever sensed that your angels were trying to _____ with you?
   Have you felt their presence surrounding you and somehow knew that God had sent them with a
   _____ _____? I've noticed that most angel communications happen during
   the late-night or early-morning hours, and that there are even specific seasons during the year when
   these spiritual lines of connection seem to be more open than at other times.

How Angels Communicate

2. Sometimes, when angels want to bring us a message, they will use _____ _____ (and
   we will discuss this later in the lesson), but generally speaking, the messages angels bring come to us
   in other ways, ways that must be recognized.

3. The first thing you need to understand is that all spiritual communication can be classified under
   one of two headings: _____ communications or _____ communications.

4. List the seven scriptural ways angels communicate with us:

   1. _____

   2. _____

   3. _____

   4. _____

5. _____

6. _____

7. _____

5. Explain in as few words as possible what we mean by angels communicating through "a knowing."

_____

_____

6. Explain in as few words as possible what we mean by angels communicating through "atmospheres."

_____

_____

7. Explain in as few words as possible what we mean by angels communicating through "signs and wonders."

_____

_____

8. Explain in as few words as possible what we mean by angels communicating through "dreams."

_____

_____

9. Explain in as few words as possible what we mean by angels communicating through "visions."

_____

_____

10. Explain in as few words as possible what we mean by angels communicating through "touch."

_____

_____

11. Explain in as few words as possible what we mean by angels communicating through "hearing."

_____

_____

Our Response to Angels and Their Messages

12. As much as your angels want to communicate with you, it is important for you to learn how to _____ _____ to them. Through my research and personal interaction with angels over the years, I've discovered that there are three initial responses that people usually have to the sudden appearance of angels in their lives.

13. Name the three most common responses people have to the appearance of angels.

_____

_____

_____

_____

14. What was your response when you saw or heard an angel?

_____

_____

AN ANGEL GIVES DIRECTIONS
by Lester Sumrall

Lester Sumrall spoke of an occasion when an angel, appearing as a person, came to the rescue for him on a mission trip overseas:

Years ago I was traveling with a group up near the border of Tibet. Somehow, I became lost—I mean absolutely lost. You know the feeling. I had been separated from my traveling companions from about 8:00 in the morning until about 4:30 that afternoon. There I was in a little Chinese village, all by myself, without knowing one word of the language. I was sad, tired, and almost in tears.

Then I noticed a young man come riding through the gates of the village on a majestic horse. He rode right up to where I was, dismounted, and began to talk to me in perfect English.

"Where did you come from?" I asked. "How is it that you speak English so beautifully?"

He smiled and said to me, "I know the party you're looking for. I met them on the road. If you go out this gate and then go for about two hours, you'll find them ahead."

I took his advice. Getting on my mule, I headed out the gate, and sure enough, before long I found the group I had been traveling with. I inquired of them about the young man. They told me they had never seen him. They didn't know anything about him. Could he have been my guardian angel? I believe he was.[11]

---

11. Lester Sumrall, *Angels to Help You* (New Kensington, PA, Whitaker House: 1999)22, p 88,

What part of this lesson stood out to you the most? How can you begin to apply this revelation to your daily life? Spend a few moments of reflection, writing down your thoughts:

_____

_____

_____

_____

_____

PART III

WORKING WITH YOUR ANGELS

"Every visible thing in this world is put in the charge of an angel."
—St. Augustine

LESSON 13

Commanding Your Angels

Before you begin this lesson, read chapter 13 in *Seeing Angels*.

…cause Your mighty ones to come down, O Lord.
—Joel 3:11

1. Over a period of many years, people would ask me, "Brother Joshua, is it okay for me to _____ my angels?" I would always answer that I didn't have a specific revelation on that subject. The only way I understood that I could interact with my angels was through _____ the Scriptures aloud, by _____ directed to God, and through focused generous _____. I knew that those three things had always activated angels in my life, and I never felt fully comfortable with the idea of commanding my angels directly.

2. In the Psalms, David says, "_____ *will command his angels*" (Psalm 91:11 CEV), and I had always felt like that was the end of the story.

3. However, everything in God is intended to be planted in our lives as a seed, and if we will allow Him to sprinkle His water (the Word) upon that seed and shine His light (the Spirit) upon it, we can expect something _____ to grow within us. And this is what happened to me in regard to commanding angels. The more I have sought God about these things, the more He has spoken to me regarding the _____ and _____ of the believer.

4. List the three principles I quoted from Kenneth Hagin's wonderful book, *The Believers Authority*, and give at least one confirming Scripture for each:

   _____

   _____

   _____

5. When I read those Scriptures as a teenager, I received an impartation of _____ _____ to move with God in the areas of healing, finances, and miracles. These Scriptures gave me great confidence, knowing that the power and authority of God resided in me through Christ Jesus. But when it came to commanding angels, I still wasn't sure, and it seemed to be a _____ subject among believers. Did I really believe that God had given us all _____ _____ _____?

6. Many believers didn't think it was possible to command angels. But wasn't that the Word of God? Had His Word to us changed? Certainly not. So, if God's Word had not changed, what needed to change?

   _____

7. Provide some biblical examples of people who commanded angels:

   _____

   _____

   _____

New Covenant Privileges

8. The Bible tells us to _____ _____ the Word (see 2 Timothy 2:15), so that we can clearly gain truthful insight of our rights and privileges in Christ. Before Jesus went to the cross, He was made a little lower than the angels (see Psalm 8:5; Hebrews 2:7). But now, on this side of the cross, He has been crowned with glory and honor, so that the angels must submit to His name. (See Hebrews 2:9; Philippians 2:10.) And look at these Scriptures:

   I also pray that you will understand the incredible greatness of God's power _____ _____ who believe him. This is the same mighty power that raised Christ from the dead and seated him in the place of honor at God's right hand in the heavenly realms. Now he is far above any ruler or authority or power or leader or anything else—not only in this world but also in the world to come.
   (Ephesians 1:19–21 NLT)

   Now Christ has gone to heaven. He is seated in the place of honor next to God, and all the angels and authorities and powers _____ _____ _____.
   (1 Peter 3:22 NLT)

9. It seems plain to see here that angels are _____ to Christ. So, let me ask you this: Where is Christ? Where does He live right now? The answer is discovered in Colossians 1:27:

   ...this is the secret: Christ lives _____ _____. This gives you assurance of sharing his _____.
   (NLT)

10. You and I have the _____ of sharing in His glory! This gives us the _____ to speak by the authority of Christ, who lives in us.

Speaking by the Authority of Christ

11. When you speak by the authority of Christ, who resides in you, the spirit world pays attention. Your words are _____, and your words are full of God's _____. When you speak by the Spirit, it is God who is speaking. (See Luke 12:12.) You must understand this.

12. Jesus said, *"Whosoever shall confess Me before men, him shall the Son of man also confess* _____ _____ _____ _____ _____" (Luke 12:8). In other words, when we confess that Jesus is our Lord, He confesses it back to the angels. He declares to them _____ _____ _____ _____. When we speak by the authority of Christ, it sets angels into action.

Who is the Commander of the Army of the Lord?

13. Since we know that many of God's angels are called "hosts" or "mighty ones," speaking in _____ _____ of a great army, the question remains: Who is the Commander of this army? Who is the Commander of the army of the Lord? We find the answer in Joshua 5:

    > *The commander of the LORD's army replied, "Take off your sandals, for the place where you are standing is holy." And Joshua did as he was told.* (Joshua 5:15 NLT)

14. In this passage, we see Joshua taking off his sandals and bowing down to worship _____ _____. This couldn't possibly have been just another angel, because throughout the Scriptures, we see that the worship of angels is forbidden, and yet Joshua seemed to be permitted to worship in this way. The Commander of the Lord's army is _____ _____, and He wants to give voice to His commands through _____ _____ ____.

15. I believe that God is telling us today the same thing that He told Moses so long ago: *"Now therefore go, and I will be with _____ _____, and teach you _____ ____ _____ ____"* (Exodus 4:12). We must have confidence that God wants to dispatch angels at our Spirit-led commands to minister for us.

    What part of this lesson stood out to you the most? How can you begin to apply this revelation to your daily life? Spend a few moments of reflection, writing down your thoughts:

    _____

    _____

    _____

    _____

    _____

Understanding Signs and Heavenly Messages

Before you begin this lesson, read chapter 14 in *Seeing Angels*.

Speak, Lord; for Your servant hears.
—1 Samuel 3:9

1. There are times when various _____ will come with the presence of angels, and the particular fragrance may indicate the ministry function or give us an understanding of the particular message our heavenly messengers are bringing to us as they administrate God's purposes in our business, ministry, or life.

2. What was the angel trying to say when we smelled baby powder in a meeting?

   _____

   _____

3. What other fragrances might be smelled, and what do they mean?

   _____

   _____

4. Through the years I have discovered that the divine supernatural realm is a "_____ realm." Once you learn how to read, perceive, and notice the signs, you will suddenly begin to encounter this realm all around you, almost everywhere you go. God loves to send us signs, tokens of His love, and I believe that He often sends them to us through the ministry of angels.

5. *But thanks be to God, who always leads us as captives in Christ's triumphal procession and uses us to spread _____ _____ of the knowledge of him everywhere.* (2 Corinthians 2:14 NIV)

This Scripture tells us clearly that God will use you and me to spread the aroma of Christ everywhere. But, since we are _____ _____ our angels, it should be no surprise that God would also choose to use the angels in this way.

ANGELS BRING SIGNS AND WONDERS
by David Herzog

My friend David Herzog has learned how to work with God's angels to release signs and wonders all over the world, and he has taught others how to do the same. In his book, *Mysteries of the Glory Unveiled*, he shared a wonderful testimony that he received in this regard:

Angels are used by God in many aspects of ministry—in healing, in signs and wonders, in protection, in communication, and in other ways as well. Angels are God's servants, and they carry out the orders of the King.

When the golden glory comes down, I always feel the presence of angels in our midst, and I know that Heaven is not very far away. All distance becomes relative in the glory.

My friend Billie Watts, the station manager of the TBN affiliate in Phoenix, Arizona, has had many experiences in this area, and often, as we have been preparing to do an interview, she has shared these experiences with me. She was also in one of the campmeetings in Ashland, where she shared an extraordinary experience.

Every evening Billie takes time to sit down at her piano and sing to the Lord. As she was worshiping Him one evening, an angel came in through her patio door and stood before her. This was no ordinary angel. Of the many angels she has seen, this one, she said, was particularly large. "Huge" was the word she used. The angel was also the first one she had seen that was solid gold.

When the angel came near to the chair where Billie was sitting, he opened his hands, and she saw golden particles falling from his fingers. After he had left, she turned on the lights to make sure what she had seen had been real. There was gold dust all over the floor, on her legs, and on the chair.

I have come to believe that every time the gold manifestations begin to appear, angels are present to precipitate it. This is why we feel the atmosphere change. The same thing happens when other signs and wonders are seen. Angels are present.[12]

"He Will Cover You with His Feathers"

6. The Scriptures declare that when you enter God's secret place, *"He will cover you _____ _____ _____"* (Psalm 91:4 NLT), and that is exactly what happened! The feathers are a sign of God covering our lives with the protection of angels.

_____

12. David Herzog, *Mysteries of the Glory Unveiled* (Shippensburg, PA: Destiny Image, 2008).

7. When our angels want to deliver a message, a very common sign they will give us is the appearance of _____. Often, these feathers are small, white, and delicate, and they will usually appear in a special place at a special time. But that's exactly the reason it grabs our attention!

8. Some people have asked me if angels really have wings with feathers, and the answer is yes, they do. The Scriptures speak about the wings of an angel. Psalm 18:10, for instance, says, *"He rode upon a cherub, and did fly, yea, He did fly _____ _____ _____ ___ ___ _____."*

9. When the psalmist considered the faithful protection of God over our lives, he sang, *"He will shelter you _____ _____ _____. His faithful promises are your armor and protection"* (Psalm 91:4 NLT).

10. Whose wings will God cover you with?

    _____

    _____

11. He has promised to cover your life with angelic protection, and He created His host of angels with you in mind. We can understand this scriptural passage more fully when we see that the psalmist later sang, *"For he will command his angels concerning you to _____ you in all your ways"* (Psalm 91:11 NIV).

12. Feathers are spiritually _____ of God's _____, _____, and _____ _____, and they help us rise above difficulties. (See Exodus 25:20; Psalm 63:7.) Feathers are also a sign that God is bringing _____ _____ to prayers and accelerating the manifestation of His blessings in your life. (See Deuteronomy 32:11.)

13. Still, some people wonder, "Can angel feathers really manifest in the natural dimension? And what do they look like?" Well, we know for certain that God chooses to release _____ _____ on the earth in a _____ sort of way. Our faith moves heaven to earth. When Jesus taught us to pray, He said to say: *"Your kingdom come. Your will be done _____ _____, as it is _____ _____"* (Matthew 6:10). So, we can see that there are times when heaven will literally begin to appear around us in the natural. That's what God desires.

14. But you may still be asking the question: "What should these feathers look like?" We can find an answer for this, once again, revealed in the Scriptures. What does Zechariah 5:9 say?

    _____

    _____

15. This revelation about the angels' wings gives us an understanding of their feathers. Therefore, when we see angel's feathers, we would expect them to look _____ _____ to the feathers of a bird. As I noted, angel feathers are often _____, but sometimes they appear to be _____ or _____ _____ altogether.

    Each color has a different prophetic symbolism, and you should apply that knowledge if and when you notice that your angel's feathers are of different colors. For that purpose, I have prepared a scriptural color chart, and it can be found in chapter 14 of the book.

16. Heavenly messages often come to us like a code, and we are given the privileged opportunity to _____ _____ their meaning. The Bible says plainly: *"It is God's privilege to _____ things and the king's privilege to _____ them"* (Proverbs 25:2 NLT). Sometimes angel feathers may even appear with an unusual pattern or in an unusual shape. One of my friends received a feather that was in a _____ formation, and the Lord spoke to him clearly through that encounter about childlike faith and the miracles it produces. It is imperative to use _____ _____ and consult _____ _____ _____ regarding each and every manifestation. We must pay attention to the signs God gives when He is sending us a message through His angels.

Angels Leave a Calling Card in New Zealand

17. One night, when we went back to our rooms after ministering in Auckland, New Zealand, what sign did the angels leave for us in the room where our son Lincoln was sleeping?

    _____

    _____

    Just weeks before that, the Lord had shown me the four angels whom He had assigned over our son, and now those angels had left their calling cards for us to find. It was another _____ _____ of a spiritual reality. Angels were watching over Lincoln.

18. God wants to show us these things, but our _____ must to be open to see them.

Decoding Angel Signs and Understanding Their Meaning

19. On face value, angel signs can be easily explained away if we don't have the _____ _____ to know that God is attempting to speak to us through these signs. Our angels want us to receive God's message, and they will do everything possible to present it to us. But, as I've shown, we must first become aware of the signs of their presence, and, second, we must take the time to ask ourselves some specific questions about those signs.

20. Name the "Six W's" an investigative journalist is taught to analyze evidence for a story and tell how they relate to *Seeing Angels*:

    _____

    _____

    _____

    _____

    _____

    _____

    _____

    _____

    _____

    _____

21. Of course, all of these questions should be asked in combination with _____ _____ and _____ _____ and through the lens of our personal relationship with Jesus Christ, in order for us to determine the full meaning of the messages we're receiving.

A Prophetic Understanding of Colors

22. In my book, *Atmosphere*,[13] I've shared about the emotional impact colors can make upon a person's physical and mental well-being, but there is also a spiritual side to the color spectrum. There is a prophetic edge that we must become aware of. Through color, God can speak to us about _____, _____ _____, _____, or any number of other things. When we begin to receive visible angel signs and messages from heaven, we should take note of the colors, textures, and patterns that we see. I have compiled a chart and inserted it here to help you understand the prophetic meaning of colors, according to the Scriptures.

23. What are the three questions we should ask ourselves when considering the colors in signs and messages from heaven?

   _____

   _____

   _____

24. Once you have started _____, you'll begin to see the angel signs and messages from heaven almost everywhere you go! Keep your spiritual senses alert, and be ready to de-code the information you receive as a gift from the glory realm!

   What part of this lesson stood out to you the most? How can you begin to apply this revelation to your daily life? Spend a few moments of reflection, writing down your thoughts:

   _____

   _____

   _____

   _____

   _____

---

13. Joshua Mills, *Atmosphere*, (Palm Springs, CA, New Wine International, 2011).

Angel Movements and Atmospheric Shifts

Before you begin this lesson, read chapter 15 in *Seeing Angels*.

You commandeered winds as messengers, appointed fire and flame as ambassadors…
—Psalm 104:4 MSG

1. Sometimes angels come as _____ _____ (see Ezekiel 37:9; John 3:8; Acts 2:2), and at other times they appear as seraphim, or servant _____ _____ _____. (See 2 Kings 2:11, 6:17; Hebrews 1:7.) You will often feel an _____ _____, even in the room temperature, when the hosts of angels begin to move in your midst. Those are the flames of fire in operation. Pray into the encounter and ask God what He is doing and how you can co-operate with Him in that moment.

2. Sometimes, when angels begin moving in your atmosphere, you will feel something _____ _____ in your hands or other parts of your physical body. At other times, you may get almost the opposite manifestation and feel absolutely _____. These are _____ _____ of something supernatural that is happening. Become sensitive to these things, and when they begin happening, ask God what He wants to reveal to you at that moment.

3. It could be that God is _____ something in your life. When He wanted to cleanse the prophet Isaiah, He sent an angel to touch his mouth with a flaming coal. (See Isaiah 6:6–7.) On the other hand, you may feel a cool breeze blowing across your fingertips as you lift your hands in worship. Thank God for His angels, who bring us refreshing encounters. When angels begin to move, you will sense them _____ _____ _____ all around you.

A BURNING BUSH
by Andrea "Andy" Mcdougal

There is a burning bush in our midst, and it is getting our attention. It is a divine visitation, and it is bringing a glory that will also loose our destinies. In fact, the greatest hour of destiny is upon the Church at this very moment.

The Angel of the LORD appeared to him in a flame of fire out of the midst of a bush.

(Exodus 3:2)

This was not any ordinary angel. This was the pre-incarnate presence of Jesus. This was the Angel of God's Presence, the Angel of the Covenant, the Angel of Jehovah, who stood right in the middle of that flame.

Now we are experiencing our own burning bush. We have been on the back side of the desert, waiting for something to take place. We have cried out to the Lord, "Fulfill our destinies," "show us Your glory," and "bring a visitation of Your presence to us." Suddenly we find ourselves under divine visitation, with the glory of God in our midst, and we realize that our destinies are about to be loosed.

Our burning bush is the visible, manifested presence of God's glory, the glory that is being displayed in the earth. The Angel of the Lord, the Angel of the Covenant, and the Angel of His Presence, is right in the middle of the glory, in the middle of the flame.

This word *flame, Strong's* (#3827 and #3851), means "a flaming head of a spear, to gleam, a flash, a sharply polished blade or point of a weapon, a blade, bright, flame, glittering." This flame was like the flaming head of a spear. It gleamed, it flashed like a sharply polished blade, and it glittered. And the Angel of the Covenant, the Angel of God's Presence, was right in the middle of this flame that gleamed, flashed, and glittered.

We are now under divine visitation, and God is manifesting His presence. It gleams, it flashes, it glitters, and the Angel of the Lord, the Angel of the Covenant, the Angel of His Presence, and the Angel of Jehovah, is right in the middle of it.[14]

Radiant Lights and Swirling Colors

4. Occasionally, the Lord allows us to encounter His angels as brilliant _____ _____. You might see an unusual spark of light in your peripheral vision, from the corner of your eye, a _____ ____ _____, or an _____ ____ _____ above you, within your field of vision. These are all indicators of angel movement around you. Pay attention to these movements and consult the Holy Spirit for His wisdom. The Bible says that God is the _____ of these heavenly lights. (See James 1:17.)

---

14. Andrea McDougal, *The Glory of God Revealed* (Greenwell Springs, LA, McDougal & Associates: 2009).

Angels Caught on Camera

5. A few years ago, I was teaching about angels at a Glory School I was hosting on the Gold Coast of Australia. Suddenly, I saw an angel appear in the back of the room and stand there against the wall. One man later testified that he had been thinking to himself, *I really wish I could see that angel. Brother Joshua said that it's right behind me.* Then he got an idea. He took out his _____ and snapped __ _____, being sure to include the area where I had said the angel was standing. He had not been able to see the angel with his natural eyes but when he looked at the photo he had taken, there it was, right behind him, exactly _____ __ _____ _____ ____ _____. He now had a selfie with an angel!

Rainbows of Light

6. Some people have the mistaken concept that _____ were only the invention of medieval artists as a way of indicating saints and angels in their paintings. Actually, the Bible speaks of real halos. We see an instance of this in Revelation 10:1:

    > Then I saw another mighty angel coming down from heaven. He was robed in a cloud, with a rainbow _____ _____ _____; his face was like the sun, and his legs were like fiery pillars.
    >
    > (Revelation 10:1 NIV)

7. What was the message of this angel, and what does it mean to you personally?

    _____

    _____

Speak It Boldly and See It Happen!

8. When signs and wonders first began happening in our ministry, several preachers told me something like, "Brother Joshua, it's wonderful that God is doing such miraculous things in your meetings, but you must only speak about Jesus. Never mention the signs." Because they were older and seemed wiser than me, and because I have always valued the importance of placing Jesus Christ above all else in both word and deed, I heeded these warnings. The problem with their advice, however, was that when we didn't speak about what God was doing, He seemed to do it less. The result was to _____ _____ _____ in our midst.

    When God gives us something, He gives it to us in _____ form, and with that seed, we are given the responsibility of finding the proper people, places, and atmospheres in which to sow it. God wants us to experience a harvest, but the only way that will happen is if and when we are willing to sow the seed He has given.

9. Eventually, the Spirit also began speaking to me about the importance of our testimony and our decrees. I saw in the Bible that an angel told John, "The _____ of Jesus is the spirit of prophecy" (Revelation 19:10). In other words, if we will be willing to speak about what God has done, that will create a door in the spirit world for Him to do it again. _____ are essential when working with angels in the glory realm. The more we speak about them, the more we will see them! Knowing this should cause us to come out from under our shells of intimidation and speak openly and often of God's marvels.

10. One evening, as I spoke about the glory of God, we watched in amazement as angels began to move in our midst. Those in attendance began pointing at something behind me. At that moment, I was standing out on the floor in front of the stage, and when I turned to see what they were pointing at, what I saw amazed me. A large and heavy curtain had been pulled across the stage. It was one of the old-fashioned kind you used to see at movie theaters. It was made of a heavy material, and yet it was _____ _____ _____ _____ with great intensity. It looked as if there was something or someone behind the curtain, pushing it back and forth violently.

Some of those present didn't consider this to be a supernatural event. They simply assumed that someone was on the stage behind the curtain, pushing it back and forth. When they went up to investigate, they were surprised to find that ____ _____ _____ _____. There were no air-conditioning vents blowing that night, and even if there had been, the air alone would not have been able to move that heavy curtain as forcefully as it was moving.

What part of this lesson stood out to you the most? How can you begin to apply this revelation to your daily life? Spend a few moments of reflection, writing down your thoughts:

_____

_____

_____

_____

_____

Spiritual Safety and Boundaries

Before you begin this lesson, read chapter 16 in *Seeing Angels*.

Dear friends, do not believe every spirit,
but test the spirits to see whether they are from God.
—1 John 4:1 (NIV)

1. The Bible gives us _____ _____ _____ regarding the spiritual beings that surround our lives on a daily basis, and I would be remiss if I did not mention it: *"Do not believe every spirit, but* _____ *the spirits…."* We must learn *how* to test the spirits, and then we must *always* test them. Some who go around talking about angels are, in actuality, encountering dark presences. These are not holy angels at all; they are fallen angels, or what we would call an _____ _____.

2. Evil spirits are spiritual beings that sometimes masquerade as _____ ___ _____. The Bible says that even Satan tries to masquerade in this way. (See 2 Corinthians 11:14.) Not every angel you meet is holy, loving, respectful, and kind. God's holy angels are _____ you, while the fallen angels are _____ you, and their intention is to do you harm. Therefore, it is important to properly understand spiritual _____ and _____ so that your experiences with angels will be pleasant, protected, peaceful, and productive.

3. Keep in mind that only _____-_____ of the angels in heaven fell with Lucifer. That means that _____-_____ of them are still working for us—and this is good news. I don't want you to be fearful; there is no need to be frightened. In this book, I've been showing you scriptural principles to help you properly connect with your angels. But the battle between good and evil is real, and

that's why we must test every spirit that comes into our presence. How can we test these spirits? It is done primarily through the gift of _____ _____ that I wrote about in chapter 9. There are, however, other indicators.

4. For instance, just as there are heavenly aromas associated with the presence of angels, likewise, there are _____ _____ associated with evil spirits. At times, you may smell them before you see them. One of the common smells associated with their dark activity is much like the stench of human or animal _____. Another aroma is similar to cigarette, cigar, or marijuana _____.

5. There are also feelings associated with the presence of evil spirits. For me, it sometimes feels like a big rubber band is being placed around my head. At other times, it feels like a sudden _____ or sharp _____. I'm not saying that those who suffer from frequent migraines or severe headaches are necessarily experiencing the presence of evil spirits, but it is certainly an evil attack, and you need to take authority over it.

6. What should you do when you feel the presence of an evil spirit?

_____

7. Just as there is a _____ _____ that comes to us when angels are present (we can feel an abundance of joy, peace, blessing, etc.), there is also an _____ _____ that sometimes comes on your chest when evil spirits are present. This feeling is not good at all and can be described as feeling suffocated.

8. When I was a child, I suffered from occasional bouts of a sudden, _____ _____. This needs a little more explanation because the presence of God's holy angels can also cause fear, as we discussed in chapter 12. A response of fear was often recorded in the Scriptures. There is a natural tendency to be afraid of anything that is unfamiliar to us. Our flesh is uncomfortable with the unfamiliar. When we experience fear, therefore, it is not necessarily an indication of an evil presence. It may well be that our flesh is learning how to deal with something new.

9. Children are extremely _____ to the presence of angels, and they are also _____ to the presence of evil spirits. As I noted, this paralyzing fear came to me as a child, and the purpose of evil spirits for bringing this on me was an attempt to short-circuit my destiny. _____ _____ your children when they talk about such encounters.

10. When we outright _____ the supernatural, it can have a negative effect on the childlike faith and trust of our loved ones.

11. What is the proper response of parents to their child's fears?

_____

_____

Detecting the Counterfeit

12. When speaking of evil spirits and their activity, the important thing is that you know _____ to look for. It's a lot like a banker, looking carefully over the money in his care to ensure that he doesn't accept anything that might be _____. In order to recognize false money, he undergoes good training that includes plenty of experience handling the real thing. Once he is accustomed to the look and feel of authentic currency, it becomes difficult for a counterfeit bill to

get past him. He knows _____ _____ from _____ _____. By spending time with the genuine, he learns what is false. Over time, his eye and his touch become extremely sensitive to the counterfeit. He knows what the real looks like, and anything else stands out like Monopoly money to him.

13. Spending more time in the presence of God's _____ and _____ on what is real will save us from experiencing much grief and tragedy. When we're in the presence of God's holiness, looking upon Jesus Christ, then, when something that is not from Him tries to enter our lives, _____ _____ go off immediately. Our alarm system begins to ring. Because we know what God is like, what _____ _____ is like, what _____ _____ says, and what _____ _____ are like, we instantly know when it's not Him, and we can take authority over the situation so that we can continue resting and enjoying the atmosphere of divine presence.

14. Spending time in the atmosphere of the Spirit is spending time in the atmosphere of _____ and _____:

    But when he, the Spirit of _____, comes, he will guide you into all the truth. He will not speak on his own; he will speak only what he hears, and he will tell you what is yet to come.

    (John 16:13 NIV)

    Then you will know the _____, and the truth will set you free.   (John 8:32 NIV)

15. Spending time in the atmosphere of _____, the atmosphere of _____, the atmosphere of _____, the atmosphere of _____, and the atmosphere of _____ trains us in the truth of who God is, and that truth _____ ____ _____ from any other thing that tries to hinder our walk with the Lord.

Boundary Lines

16. Define a boundary line:

    _____

17. Understanding the _____ _____ is necessary if you want to remain in safe territory. There is a protection line in the spirit world, and that line is the Word of God.

18. Mary K. Baxter has shared: "Not all angels are kind and benevolent. There are good angels and there are evil angels. Good angels continually seek to do God's will, and they work for our benefit. Evil angels seek ____ _____ ____ about their true intentions toward us. They are demons who want ____ _____ ____ rather than help us. This is why it can be very dangerous to learn about angels from those who don't have a solid biblical understanding of their true nature and ways."

19. Although the supernatural world is very vast and wide, any spiritual reality outside of God's Word can lead to _____, _____, and ultimate _____. Jesus declared, *"Enter through the narrow gate. For wide is the gate and broad is the road that leads to _____, and many enter through it. But small is the gate and narrow the road that leads to life, and only a few find it"* (Matthew 7:13–14 NIV). We must remain within the boundaries of God's Word. When we do this, we will also be covered by the protective _____ of Jesus and the blessing of the Holy Spirit. Divine angels honor God and His Word.

Fallen Angels

20. Peter informed us that, when certain angels sinned, God *"cast them down to hell, and delivered them into chains of _____, to be reserved to _____"* (2 Peter 2:4). In the same manner, Jude stated, *"The angels which kept not their first estate, but left their own habitation, He has reserved in _____ _____ under darkness to the judgment of the great day"* (Jude 1:6), where these angels will suffer *"the vengeance of _____ _____"* (verse 7). Jesus declared that this everlasting fire was *"prepared for the devil and his angels"* (Matthew 25:41).

21. There is ____ _____ for the fallen angels, and they _____ ____ _____. This is why the holy angels are said to mysteriously desire to look into matters of salvation and redemption. (See 1 Peter 1:10–12.) Only humans can testify to the amazing grace of Christ as the Holy Spirit reveals it to us. In the same way that *"Satan himself masquerades as an angel of light"* (2 Corinthians 11:14 NIV), these fallen angels, as evil spirits, sometimes _____ __ _____ _____ as good spirits, when in reality, they are foul, dark, and impure.

22. What are a few of the many names given to fallen angels in the Scriptures?

    _____

    _____

    _____

    _____

    _____

    _____

    _____

    _____

23. What are some ways we can recognize fallen angels?

    _____

    _____

    _____

    _____

Boundaries for Angels

24. List a few of the boundaries set by God for His angels:

    _____

    _____

    _____

25. List three tests that can be used for all angel encounters.

_____

_____

_____

26. Through this book, you've received instruction from the Word that has imparted enough faith for this realm to open fully for you. Now, it's time to pay close attention to the movement of angels around you. What do you see?

_____

_____

_____

_____

What part of this lesson stood out to you the most? How can you begin to apply this revelation to your daily life? Spend a few moments of reflection, writing down your thoughts:

_____

_____

_____

_____

_____

Answer Key

Lesson 1

1. commissioned; specific tasks

2. angels of protection, deliverance, and comfort; angels of healing; angels of abundant provision; angels of divine love; angels on extraordinary assignment; angels of breakthrough and revival; angels over churches, cities, and nations

3. specific angels

4. messenger from God; ambassador; to dispatch as a deputy

5. messenger; sent one

6. LIST YOUR OWN EXPERIENCES.

7. large groups; armies; chariots; hosts; holy; company; sons; stars; watchers

8. GIVE YOUR OWN ANSWER

9. forgive sins; judge the earth; receive worship

10. higher; one; only Son of God; worship Him; created; existed; eternity

11. Gabriel

12. not God; an angel

13. two; four; six; face; hands; feet

14. eyes

15. GIVE YOUR OWN DESCRIPTIONS AND THEN CHECK THEIR ACCURACY WITH THE BOOK.

16. spirit beings; spirit bodies

17. agression; strength; authority

18. nurture; love; wisdom

19. 1. Seraphim; Cherubim; Thrones. 2. Dominions; Virtues; Powers. 3. Principalities; Archangels; Ministering Spirits; COMPARE YOUR DESCRIPTIONS WITH THE BOOK.

20. I can see angels in the Bible because God has given them a place, plan, and purpose in the Scriptures! I can also see angels in my life because God has given them a place, plan, and purpose for me! The angels follow God's precepts, as they point me toward Jesus Christ! I follow God's precepts, as I point others toward Jesus Christ! As I begin *Seeing Angels*, I will keep my focus on all that God has commanded me to do!

Lesson 2

1. protection; deliverance

2. throne; attendants

3. decree; declare; servants; instructions; angels; instructions

4. GIVE YOUR OWN ANSWER.

5. angels; they

6. GIVE YOUR OWN ANSWER.

7. through you and me

8. THERE ARE MANY. GIVE YOUR OWN EXAMPLES.

9. GIVE YOUR OWN ANSWER

10. Gabriel

11. GIVE YOUR OWN ANSWER

12. quickly dismissing their ministry

13. God's Word; God's angels

14. family members; loved ones; peace; possessions; property; finances; inheritance; ministry; the anointing

15. GIVE YOUR OWN ANSWER

16. problems; His angels; good times; bad times

17. angels; alleviate the stress; strengthen us; disruptions; angels

18. God was commanding His angels to comfort His people.

19. the enemy; peace; tranquility

Lesson 3

1. heaven; earth; healing; homes; workplaces; schools; ministries; healing; miracles

2. organs; tissue; blood cells; bones; strained torn muscles

3. four angels; angel of healing; Raphael; healing virtues

4. Michael; Gabriel; Lucifer; Abaddon or Appollyon

5. Raphael; Healing One of God

6. Doctor of medicine; medicines; cures from evil spirits; stirred up; Pool of Bethesda

7. gift of healing; encounters; healing angels

8. now; in all of history; Revelation; angel encounters

9. His ministering spirits; Great Physician; nurse practitioners

10. healing angels X 2; new wine

11. new wine; direct infusion

12. ministering spirits

13. GIVE YOUR OWN DESCRIPTION.

14. *"He heals the broken in heart, and binds up their wounds."* (NLT)

15. heart; heart-healing

16. deep guilt; shame; regret; rejection; past wounds

Lesson 4

1. Prosperity

2. Jesus

3. prosperity; financial replenishment; abundant wealth; overflow

4. GIVE YOUR OWN ANSWER

5. GIVE YOUR OWN ANSWER

6. angels of blessing

7. money miracles

8. generous giving; speaking

9. change

10. financial condition

11. provisions

12. always plenty left; angels of prosperity

13. bend physical laws

14. natural; supernatural; possible; impossible

15. direct connection

Lesson 5

1. true and meaningful love

2. alone; helper

3. angels; angels of divine love

4. romantic relationship; maintaining; bring; keep

5. GIVE YOUR OWN ANSWER

6. GIVE YOUR OWN ANSWER

7. performing God's will for you; proper mate

8. Abraham; He would send an angel; accustomed; absolutely sure

9. ministry of angels

10. drawn to you

11. uptight; stressed out; nit-picky; constantly concerned with unimportant details

12. GIVE YOUR OWN ANSWER

13. encourage; treasure; positive, uplifting words

14. speaking; blessings; promises

15. everything wonderful

16. repent; quick to forgive; make room

17. GIVE YOUR OWN ANSWER

18. individually in Christ; as a team; with Him; as a couple; angels

19. (1) a lack of spending time together in God's Word, (2) a lack of praying together as a couple, (3) a lack of generously sharing intimate time together

Lesson 6

1. could

2. not to remove your own personal responsibility; impossible; possible

3. can; responsibility; lazy; efficient; effective; intervene

4. answered; never covered with shame; encamps around; delivers

5. prayers; ever ready; carrying out His purposes

6. many types

7. to strengthen them; supernatural food; forty; forty

8. charged; find treasured things; finding angels; personal keepsakes; misplaced files or documents; missing household items; inheritances; lost people

9. angels; family heirloom; given you

10. find us a perfect parking space; always knows best

Lesson 7

1. personal health; finances; family situations; ministries; businesses; workplace and school situations; sudden turnarounds

2. pray; speak the Word of God boldly; resistance; anxiety; fear, God's Word of breakthrough

3. appeared; woke him up

4. unexpected; suddenlies

5. Quick; get up

6. don't resist; don't hold back; obedience

7. instructions; direct; ministry assignments; His; written Word; confirmation

8. specific assignment

9. Move; move; move

10. breakthrough angel; heaven

11. angels of harvest; sickle; reap; time to reap; ripe

12. commissioned; a harvest of the nations; the angels of harvest

13. His angels; complacent; passionately pursue

14. released with ease

15. The pastor informed me that he didn't believe in divine healing, the current reality of miracles, or God's ability to prosper His people. The Spirit-filled pastor who had invited me had retired, and this man, who was not Spirit-filled, had taken his place.

16. No, in spite of the pastor and his preconceived ideas of what could and could not happen today, miracles happened, healings took place, and supernatural finances were released. God did everything that pastor didn't believe in!

17. glory; different

18. Swift; He brings acceleration to prophetic fulfillment.

19. bring direction

20. many different forms; unusual; supernatural

21. Oil flowing from my head, hands, and feet; Two cups overflowing with oil appearing in my room; My Bible moving from where I had left it; Its pages being covered with gold dust; The Bible being opened to Revelation 5 as a confirmation of what God had spoken to me; The worship leader seeing lights flashing and bouncing around his room all night; My hands again flowing with oil; The people experiencing physical healings and emotional breakthroughs; The worship leader falling to the floor, overcome by the power of the Spirit; The keyboard continuing to play on its own accord; Angels singing in our midst

22. Intensified glory

23. outpouring; revival

Lesson 8

1. church; city; nation

2. apostles; prophets; evangelists; teachers; ministry concerns; finances; church assignments; help local pastors

3. chapter 2; chapter 3

4. pastors; bishops; the angels of the seven churches

5. addressed to; congregations; for; the delivery agents

6. protection; guidance; strength; victory; church

7. mine angel

8. city of angels; the angels; atmosphere; fiery furnace; ambush; in her old age; conceive; Christ's birth; Jesus was alive; return of Christ; prepared the atmosphere

9. principalities; powers; rulers; spiritual darkness

10. holy; fallen

11. prayer; intercession; decrees

12. supervising angel

13. rulers; principalities; dominions; powers; emanating from

14. armor of God; plans; assignments; attacks

15. the glory; rest

16. captive; oppressed

17. I Daniel alone; holiness

18. to change you; city; territory; region

19. trembling; Greece; Persia; Israel; fallen; holy

20. individual nations; the angels of the nations

21. Victoricus

22. specific purpose and call

23. influence nations, shift atmospheres; change cultures

Lesson 9

1. He helped them financially and encouraged them to stand strong in faith.

2. glory realms

3. Great Shepherd; comfort; peace; Jesus

4. discern; distinguish between; holy; profane; godly; flesh; God; enemy

5. blind; dimmed

6. surround your life

7. An angel spoke to her in a restaurant and assured her that she would soon be seeing the wonders of God.

8. fear; mindset; boundaries; their own perceptions

9. we don't perceive them; discern

10. the Scriptures

11. Spiritual enlightenment, spiritual clarity, and spiritual awareness; COMPARE YOUR ANSWER TO THE SECOND PART OF THE QUESTION WITH THE BOOK.

12. heart; head

13. natural; supernatural; unseen; eternal

14. unseen

15. in part 2X; partial; incomplete; part

16. gift; discipline; trained themselves

17. enlightenment; clarity; awareness

18. spiritual realities

Lesson 10

1. normal

2. I was rebuked by my elders for saying that I had seen angels.

3. like little children

4. childlike faith

5. childlike faith

6. son, trainee

7. confident; awe-inspired; discovering; expectant; tenacious

8. CHECK YOUR ANSWER AGAINST THE BOOK.

9. CHECK YOUR ANSWER AGAINST THE BOOK.

10. CHECK YOUR ANSWER AGAINST THE BOOK.

11. CHECK YOUR ANSWER AGAINST THE BOOK.

12. CHECK YOUR ANSWER AGAINST THE BOOK.

13. childlike faith

14. the inner operations of your mind

15. imagined

16. joy

17. the faculty of imagining, or of forming mental images or concepts of what is not actually present to the senses

18. vain

19. every high thing; consecrated; submission

20. in physical form; in visions; in dreams; CHECK YOUR ANSWER TO THE SECOND PART OF THE QUESTION AGAINST THE BOOK.

21. GIVE YOUR OWN ANSWER.

22. GIVE YOUR OWN ANSWER.

23. She gave us the information we needed to minister to a celebrity we saw performing on the street, who later was seated at the table next to us in a restaurant.

24. in a dream

Lesson 11

1. Goodness; Mercy

2. my son's guardian angel; I was surprised because Lincoln, a toddler at the time, had been saying that angels name for some time and we hadn't realized it was the name of an angel.

3. God Is Judge

4. final word

5. name; relationship

6. bring glory to themselves

7. Wonderful; Healing; Deliverance; Harvest; Glory

8. a warrior angel

9. to bring prophetic acceleration

10. Caramat was assigned to bring creative miracles and signs and wonders, Zimri was assigned to bring forth the new song, and Ryan was assigned to bring me holy boldness and strength.

11. GIVE YOUR OWN ANSWER.

12. just before going to sleep or after waking up; when you are restful

13. Watchful and Alert; a watcher angel

Lesson 12

1. communicate; special message

2. their voices

3. subtle; overt

4. by a knowing; by atmospheres; by signs and wonders; by dreams; by visions; by touch; by hearing

5. CHECK YOUR ANSWER AGAINST THE BOOK

6. CHECK YOUR ANSWER AGAINST THE BOOK

7. CHECK YOUR ANSWER AGAINST THE BOOK

8. CHECK YOUR ANSWER AGAINST THE BOOK

9. CHECK YOUR ANSWER AGAINST THE BOOK

10. CHECK YOUR ANSWER AGAINST THE BOOK

11. CHECK YOUR ANSWER AGAINST THE BOOK

12. properly respond

13. Some become fearful; some are emotionally impacted; some remain calm

14. GIVE YOUR OWN ANSWER

Lesson 13

1. command; decreeing; prayer; giving

2. God

3. new; rights; authority

4. 1) In Christ, all spiritual blessings belong to us (Ephesians 1:3). 2) When Christ ascended, He transferred His authority to the Church. He is the Head of the Church, and believers make up the Body (Matthew 28:18 and Luke 10:19). 3) Christ is seated at the right hand of the Father—the place of authority—and we are seated with Him (Ephesians 2:4-6).

5. bold faith; controversial; power and authority

6. my understanding of it

7. CHECK YOUR ANSWER AGAINST THE BOOK

8. rightly divide; for us; accept his authority

9. subject; in you; glory

10. privilege; right

11. powerful; authority

12. before the angels of God; what we have declared

13. military terms

14. the Commander; Jesus Himself; you and me

15. your mouth; you shall say

Lesson 14

1. fragrances

2. In the natural, for a couple that wanted children, that babies were on the way. In the spiritual, for anyone hungry for more, that new things were coming.

3. I mentioned here fire burning, signifying sacrifice and roses, signifying Christ. In another part of the book, I mentioned musk, speaking of loving attraction. You may experience many others.

4. signs

5. the aroma; partnered with

6. with his feathers

7. feathers

8. upon the wings of the wind

9. with his wings

10. the wings of His angels

11. guard

12. symbolic; faithfulness; protection; covenant promise; swift answers

13. spiritual realities; natural; in earth; in heaven

14. *"they had wings like a stork"* (NLT)

15. very similar; white; black; another color

16. search out; conceal; discover; spiral; godly discernment; the Holy Spirit

17. four feathers perfectly arranged side-by-side on his chest; natural indicator

18. eyes

19. prophetic understanding

20. <u>W</u>ho, <u>W</u>hat, <u>W</u>here, <u>W</u>hen, <u>W</u>hy, and Ho<u>w</u>? CHECK YOUR ANSWERS ON HOW THEY RELATE TO *SEEING ANGELS* WITH THE BOOK.

21. spiritual discernment; common sense

22. healing; spiritual growth; redemption

23. 1) What is my personal connection to this color? (i.e. Personal memories, past experiences, or emotional attachments, etc.) 2) How does this color make me feel? (i.e. It brings me joy, excitement, comfort, or peace, etc.) 3) What do the Scriptures say about this color, and how does it apply to my current situation?

24. looking

Lesson 15

1. spirit winds; flames of fire; atmospheric shift

2. like electricity; numb; natural indicators

3. purifying; shifting the atmosphere

4. shining lights; flash of lightning; orb of light; Father

5. camera; a selfie; where I had said it was

6. halos; above his head

7. No more delay; GIVE YOUR OWN ANSWER.

8. limit the miracles; seed

9. testimony; testimonies

10. swaying back and forth; no one was there

Lesson 16

1. very specific instructions; test; evil spirit

2. angels of light; for; against; safety; boundaries

3. one third; two thirds; discerning spirits

4. foul aromas; feces; smoke

5. migraine; headache

6. tell it to leave in Jesus's name

7. heavenly weightiness; ungodly heaviness

8. paralyzing fear

9. sensitive 2X; listen to

10. dismiss

11. Teach them God's promises of protection, speak those promises over them, and have them learn the promises for themselves.

12. what; counterfeit; the real; the false

13. glory; focusing; warning bells; His presence; His Word; His works

14. purity; truth; truth; truth

15. truth; purity; faith; anointing; glory; sets us free

16. something that indicates bounds or limits

17. boundary lines

18. to deceive us; to harm us

19. pain; devastation; tragedy; destruction; blood

20. darkness; judgment; everlasting chains; eternal fire

21. no grace; cannot be redeemed; attempt to present themselves

22. deaf and mute spirit (Mark 9:25); spirit of deception (1 Kings 22:21); spirit of distress (1 Samuel 16:15); spirit of Egypt (Isaiah 19:3); spirit of falsehood (Micah 2:11); spirit of harlotry (Hosea 4:12); spirit of heaviness (Isaiah 61:3); spirit of ill-will (Judges 9:23); spirit of infirmity or sickness (Luke 13:11); spirit of lies (1 Kings 22:23); spirit of perversion (Isaiah 19:14); spirit of uncleanliness (Zechariah 13:2; Matthew 12:43)

23. Fallen angels always lie. God and His angels never lie, but, instead, they lead us into truth.; Fallen angels will present you with a message that is contrary to God's Word. True angels will direct you to God's Word.; Fallen angels will draw you to themselves and away from God. God's angels work for Him and will always point you toward seeing Jesus, high and exalted on the throne of your heart.; Fallen angels will lead you away from a life in the Spirit and corrupt you with a desire for carnal things. God's angels do the opposite.

24. Angels do not live inside of us; We do not work for angels; Angels are not called to preach or teach God's Word.

25. 1) the revelation; 2) the recognition; 3) the results

26. GIVE YOUR OWN PERSONAL ANSWER.

Recommended Resources:

Books by Joshua Mills:
- ✦ *Encountering Your Angels: Biblical Proof That Angels Are Here to Help*
- ✦ *Moving in Glory Realms: Exploring Dimensions of Divine Presence*
- ✦ *Seeing Angels: How to Recognize and Interact with Your Heavenly Messengers*

Audios by Joshua Mills (CD & Digital Download):
- ✦ Activating Angels in Your Life: Angelic Activations and Heavenly Encounters
- ✦ Experience His Glory
- ✦ SpiritSpa: Instrumental Piano
- ✦ SpiritSpa 2

Books by Other Authors:
- ✦ *A Divine Revelation of Angels* by Mary K. Baxter
- ✦ *The Angel Book* by Charles and Frances Hunter
- ✦ *Everyday Angels* by Charity Kayembe and Joe Brock
- ✦ *The Glory of God Revealed* by Andrea McDougal
- ✦ *God of Wonders* by Brian Guerin
- ✦ *Miracles That I Have Seen* by William A. Ward
- ✦ *Mysteries of the Glory Unveiled* by David Herzog
- ✦ *Storm Warrior* by Mahesh and Bonnie Chavda
- ✦ *Heaven and the Angels* by H.A. Baker
- ✦ *Angels to Help You* by Lester Sumrall

Joshua Mills' resources are available online at:
www.JoshuaMills.com